What People Are Saying About
My Soul Said to Me . . .

"*My Soul Said to Me* is a dramatic story of both personal and social transformation. Bob Roberts is one of the few prophetic voices of our time who can inspire us to more effective, cooperative, compassionate action on behalf of those who have had no advocates."

—Robert Moore, Ph.D.
Jungian analyst and author, *The Archetype of Initiation: Sacred Space, Ritual Process and Personal Transformation* and *Facing the Dragon: Confronting Personal and Spiritual Grandiosity*

"As governor of Louisiana in the early 1980s, I became exceedingly alarmed about our steadily increasing prison population and our very high rate of recidivism. Although some measures were enacted that targeted these problems, they continued to grow. What was desperately needed was a program of after-care for released prisoners. We were blessed by the appearance about eight years ago of Dr. Bob Roberts, who gave up a comfortable life as a successful dentist to take on this challenge. This book chronicles a unique journey that has been successful in its goal of giving guidance and hope to hundreds of ex-convicts, leading many to productive lives and reducing the rate of recidivism. It is a truly inspiring story."

—David C. Treen
Louisiana's first Republican governor since Reconstruction

"Bob Roberts' story is an incredibly moving and inspiring account of how one concerned man can make a huge difference in so many people's lives. He is certainly a key player in the reform movement. His healing model is both effective and replicable, and goes right to the heart of the matter. This book is a must-read for anyone interested in prison reform and human potential—real heart stuff."

—Richard Gere
actor and activist

"Part personal memoir and part narrative of a groundbreaking prison literacy program, this book will probably be compared to Helen Prejean's *Dead Man Walking.* . . . Roberts' emotional attachment to his work is evident in his strong, evocative writing . . . this worthwhile, important book offers a bright, optimistic window into the often horrific conditions that still exist in prisons today . . ."

D0190177

"Our prisons are training camps in degradation, corruption and vicious violence. They disgrace our nation and endanger its future, because the criminal 'justice' system and the behavior and values learned in prisons determine the education of millions of the nation's children and youth. This book tells of one man's courage 'to do something about it.' As well, it challenges the courage of us readers to face our passive complicity that perpetuates the system. Roberts' personal account of step-by-step awakening—or 'behavior modification'—in himself and the inmates he worked with places this book in our great and noble tradition of reform.

—**James Hillman**
author, *The Soul's Code: In Search of Character and Calling*

"It takes boldness, determination and an acute sense of service to the world in pain to do what Bob Roberts has done. His journey speaks to all souls who have heard the call to live at the edge courageously and sacrificially. To leave a cozy, well-remunerated profession for one that promises nothing but bad news, uncertainty and threat is to subscribe to recklessness. But Bob Roberts heard his call and responded wholeheartedly to it, setting an example for all of us. This testimony should be read with the heart and held as evidence that playing it safe in life is disrespectful to our purpose."

—**Malidoma Somé**
author, *Of Water and the Spirit: Ritual, Magic, and Initiation
in the Life of an African Shaman*

"This book could have been called *The Soul in and out of Prison*. Robert Roberts gave up an easy, untroubled life in order to experience what happens to men and women in prison. When he saw what that was, he worked to change it. This is a passionate, sobering story that paradoxically brings hope into dark places of the American psyche."

—**Robert Bly**
author, *Iron John: A Book About Men*

"I like books that trace a journey and show a seemingly impossible dream coming true. I was privileged to participate in the community circle of Project Return once, and I grasped immediately the source for its success—community. People gathered together, vulnerable, connecting to each other, finding their voices and sharing their lives in simple honesty. This story is a refreshing testimony but it's also a roadmap to community and healing. And, most importantly, it's a bright and gleaming sign of possibility that will inspire others to create ways to reach out and include the "least of these" which our society tends to throw away."

—**Sister Helen Prejean**
author, *Dead Man Walking*

MY SOUL SAID TO ME

An Unlikely Journey Behind the Walls of Justice

Robert E. Roberts
D.D.S., Ph.D., M.S.W.

Health Communications, Inc.
Deerfield Beach, Florida

www.hci-online.com

"Walking Through a Wall" from *An Almost Human Gesture* ©1987 by Louis Jenkins. Used by permission of the poet.

"A Foolish Project," "The Guest House" and "The Question" by Rumi from *The Essential Rumi*, translations by Coleman Barks ©1995.

"Oh, My Friend" from *Mirabai Versions* by Robert Bly, Red Ozier Press, ©1984. Used by permission of Robert Bly.

"The Wind One Brilliant Day" from *Times Alone: Selected Poems of Antonio Machado*, translated by Robert Bly, Wesleyan University Press, ©1983. Used by permission of Robert Bly.

"The Man Watching" from *Selected Poems by Rainer Maria Rilke*, a translation by Robert Bly, ©1981. Used by permission of Robert Bly.

"The Journey" by Mary Oliver. From DREAM WORK by Mary Oliver. ©1986 by Mary Oliver. Used by permission of Grove/Atlantic, Inc.

"Kindness" from *Words Under the Words: Selected Poems* by Naomi Shihab Nye, ©1995. Reprinted with the permission of Far Corner Books.

"Loaves and Fishes" from *The House of Belonging* by David Whyte. ©1997 by David Whyte. Used by permission of the author and of Many Rivers Press.

"The Well of Grief" from *Where Many Rivers Meet* by David Whyte. ©1990 by David Whyte. Used by permission of the author and of Many Rivers Press.

Library of Congress Cataloging-in-Publication Data

Roberts, Robert E.

My soul said to me : an unlikely journey behind the walls of justice / Robert E. Roberts.

p. cm.

ISBN 0-7573-0064-2

1. Social workers–Louisiana–Biography.   2. Social work with criminals–Louisiana.   3. Prisons–Louisiana.   4. Prisons–United States.   I. Title.

HV28.R545 A3 2003

365'.66–dc21

2002032938

Publisher: Health Communications, Inc.
3201 S.W. 15th Street
Deerfield Beach, FL 33442-8190

Cover design by Larissa Hise Henoch
Inside book design by Lawna Patterson Oldfield
Cover photo ©Digital Vision

Contents

Acknowledgments

*M*y soul took me on this journey, but many other souls guided me through. To those who helped me write this book, I wish to express my deep gratitude. The initial "shove" came from Dr. Peter Soderburgh at LSU, who signed off on my dissertation, walked me into his office and insisted that I immediately begin writing it. Joy Parker, my dedicated editor and friend, taught me how to put it together, told me I could write, kept me from getting discouraged and saw me through the traps. My literary agent is Bonnie Solow. Her confidence and conviction that this story was worth the weeks and months I spent writing it these last six years were as valuable as her savvy in the publishing business. The final manuscript resulted from the generous efforts of poets Tim Young and Thomas Smith, and also writer Tom Devine whose dedicated friendship and input were inestimable in value. Finally, Christine Belleris of Health Communications, Inc., had the insight to understand the message and Peter Vegso the boldness to publish it.

To write this story, I needed solitude as much as anything. An old neighbor and friend from Shreveport, Gerry Huggs, allowed me to spend numerous days at his seaside home, Sea Vista, in Depoe Bay, while on working trips to Oregon. Without Gerry's kindness, I do not think I could have completed the manuscript. We lost him last year and I still miss him.

Many of the stories within were told through the courageousness of the men who, in spite of retribution by prison staff, participated in the research we conducted at Dixon Correctional Institute in Jackson, Louisiana. They are always in my prayers.

I must convey honor and gratitude to my trusted friend, teacher and mentor, Malidoma Somé, whose exceptional wisdom often kept my uncertainty from becoming despair. The generosity of other teachers guided me through the most difficult times—they are Spencer Murray, Doug Greve, M.D., Robert Bly, Dr. James Hillman, Dr. Robert Moore, Haki Madhubuti, Martin Prechtel, Dr. Aaron Kipnis, M. Scott Peck, M.D., Sister Helen Prejean, Miguel Rivera, Rowena Pentaleon, Ted Duncan, drummer Luther Gray and Mama Jamilla.

My deepest thanks go to John Densmore (drummer for the Doors) and his lovely wife, Leslie Neale, who brought forth their talents, compassion, courage and personal finances to create a documentary film about the participants and mission of Project Return.

My brilliant board of directors is made up of dedicated supporters and advisors who see our work as simply a way of breaking the cycles of crime without doing further harm. They are chairman David Hunt, Raphael Goyeneche, Earl Bihlmeyer, former Louisiana Governor David Treen, Dan Dreiling, Roger Peck, Mitty Terrel, Mike Sanderson, Barbara Lachenmaier, Betsie Gambel, Herschel Abbott, Harry Lowenburg, Eustis Reily, Joan Coulter, Allen Favrot, Ed Morris, Rev. Dwight Webster, city councilman Oliver Thomas, Lois Lawrence and Laurie White.

A few special friends: Thomas Albrecht, born about one hour before me, came into my life from the U.S. Department of Justice. If ever two people came here together from the Spirit World intending to work as partners, it is Tom and I. So different and yet so connected are this man and I. Doug Von Koss came into my life from the San Francisco Opera and taught me to love singing again. Oh, the singing! Helen Mumm, my amazing mother-in-law, whom I also lost last year, cheered me on even during the times when her own life was hardly bearable. Former Louisiana Governor David C. Treen, certainly the best and most honorable governor Louisiana has ever known, walked me through the halls of the Capitol on numerous occasions to keep our work alive. Christine Westfeldt, a truly generous woman, who made the first contribution and many others to Project Return. Phil Matthews of Blackrock Foundation, and Michael Sanderson of Second Chance Foundation, whose generosity has seen eight of Project Return's graduates through to college degrees. Dr. Richard Sutton, a trusted friend from the Department of Justice in Washington, D.C. My annual men's group in Minnesota: Phil Norrgard, Richard Scott, Doug Padilla, Jack Gundersen (world-class singer and snorer), David Gros, Dr. Will Winter, Craig Ungerman, Steve Jensen and writer/poet Brad Fern. Dr. Earl Cheek, who did not believe my research hypothesis could be proven, but supported me throughout the process anyway. The members of the New Orleans Business Council. Members of the Louisiana State Legislature: Senator Tom Schedler, Senate President John Hainkel, Senator Ken Hollis. And, lastly, Sheriff Mike Neustrom of Lafayette Parish, truly a one-of-a-kind Louisiana sheriff.

The members of my staff at Project Return share many characteristics, not the least of which is heroism. Many of them carry the scars of poverty, violence, neglect, miseducation and incarceration. If ever a study is conducted on the human resource of endurance and resilience, better subjects could not be found than Perry Bernard, Rochelle Perry, Cecile Scorza, John Mehlhorn, J. C. Greenberry, John Lewis, Dennis Gabriel, Susan Perniciaro, Leonard Morris, Perry Barbarin, Rosalind Clark, Bethany Cupit, Toshiba DeJean, Roderick Doakes, Russell Gardner, Justin Givson, James Gorczyk, Donna King and Jim O'Neill.

I could write a complete book about my sons, Bob, Jeff, Adam and Joel, and their courage throughout the last twelve or so years in standing their own ground, seeking their own path, overcoming their wounds and achieving lives of integrity, dignity, self-reliance and dedication to making this a better world. What a joy it would be to someday write that book. My mother, Armenta, and stepfather, Clyde Hollenshead, thought I had lost my mind when I left my practice of dentistry, loved me anyway, and later, understood.

My wife, Rosemary Mumm (Rosie) is a better writer, braver, funnier, as loving, straightforward and trustworthy as anyone known to me. The greatest test and the greatest fun in writing this book came when she read it through, tidied a few things up, and said she loved it. I love her.

The wind, one brilliant day, called
to my soul with an aroma of jasmine.
"In return for the odor of my jasmine,
I'd like the odor of your roses."
"I have no roses; all the flowers
in my garden are dead."
"Well then, I'll take the withered petals
and the yellow leaves and the waters of the fountain."
The wind left. And I wept. And my soul said to me:
"What have you done with the garden that was entrusted to you?"

ANTONIO MACHADO
TRANSLATED BY ROBERT BLY

Author's Note

*T*he names of several individuals have been altered for reasons of confidentiality.

CHAPTER

1

Seeds of Transformation

O n the first day of the first workshop I had ever conducted in a prison, my colleague, Rusty Meyers, and I
were unavoidably nervous as the circle gathered. We were
going behind locked doors for two and a half days to face a
group, chosen by lottery, of fifty male prisoners, most of
them black. This gathering of prisoners included murderers,
rapists, small- and big-time drug dealers, and men serving
life sentences for other serious crimes. Furthermore, we were
there to conduct a three-year study and would ask them to
cooperate fully in a group process called community building, a concept that was foreign even to most people on the
"outside."

As I walked—my mouth a bit dry—into the large, stark room, I noticed video cameras in each corner. Colonel Daniel Aucoin, a black deputy chief of security, accompanied us into the room to show that we had top-level support. He had suggested that we take emergency radio transmitters with us in case violence broke out. We had declined. Why we declined, I do not know to this day, other than to say that our gut told us we wouldn't need them. Aware that we were improvising each step of the way, we also declined video surveillance. We had no experience in making these kinds of decisions; none of us had ever tried anything like this before.

Colonel Aucoin instructed the prisoners to make themselves a nametag and to take a chair in the circle. After that, he walked out and closed the door behind him. The room was quiet. Suddenly, five of the men bolted from their chairs and swiftly disappeared out the door. Though attendance at this gathering was mandatory, for these five, sitting in a circle where fifty other faces could be seen all at the same time was too intense, even if skipping out meant a trip to "the dungeon" (solitary confinement). I had been forewarned that this would happen, and afterward I made sure that the men were not punished for a reaction they could not help.

Rusty and I introduced ourselves and briefly explained why we were there. Rusty was formerly a corporate banker from Kansas City who, like me, had set aside his career to follow a different voice. He was trained by Dr. M. Scott Peck to lead community-building workshops. Dr. Peck recommended him to me as the best and most experienced leader in the country. When I contacted Rusty about working on this research project, though, I learned that he and his wife had recently resettled in Maine to build homes with his brother-in-law. It was a job that would allow him some time to pursue his talents as a workshop leader. However, when I told him that we would be conducting the research inside a prison, he readily accepted the challenge even though it meant commuting biweekly to Louisiana.

As the process began, we did not reveal to the group who we were specifically, nor for whom we worked. Our immediate purpose, we explained to them, was to build community with those present.

There was a large spread in the ages among the group's members, ranging from sixteen into the sixties. Paranoia, fear and complaining were rampant as the men fired questions at us. They accused us of trying to use them as guinea pigs or, more specifically, that we had come there to "fuck with their heads." The night before, to assist the men in their task of becoming this thing we called a community, we had distributed throughout their dormitory a letter of vague explanations. Now, as in these workshops on the outside, we read to them a list of guidelines for successful community building[1] and then gave them three minutes of silence to contemplate the letter and the guidelines. At the end of the silence, we would announce, "You may begin."

This brief period was like the split seconds a person experiences before a skidding car wreck, those moments when one's entire life passes before him or her. Instead of my life's scenes, however, I heard my life's questions charging through my mind. *How the hell did I ever get here? What the hell am I doing here? Why have I walked away from my career—a lucrative, successful dental practice—and why did I turn my back on all those difficult (and expensive) years in college? Why have I left a marriage of twenty-four years, which gave me four beautiful sons? Why have I left the hometown where I grew up and a lifetime of friends? What the hell have I come to and where am I going?* Toward the end of those three minutes, an answer, although vague, came to me, easing my troubled questioning a bit: *Because you belong here in this circle.*

I had only visited a prison one other time, a few years earlier. That was during the tail end of a very wild and foolish period of my life during which I drove race cars and flew stunt planes for a hobby. A friend, Wellborn Jack, with whom I owned a sailplane, had asked me to fly him down to Angola, home of Louisiana's State Penitentiary. As the nation's largest maximum-security prison, Angola covers eighteen thousand acres of plantation land on the banks of the Mississippi River and has a population of five thousand prisoners. Wellborn was a criminal defense attorney and he needed to interview a witness at Angola in preparation for a trial.

"Sure," I said. "Sounds exciting. I've never been to a prison. Oughta be interesting." There was an airstrip on the prison grounds where we could land the two-passenger stunt plane that I flew in local air shows. "We'll go down there right side up and come back upside down," I quipped.

A few days later, I landed my star-studded Super Decathlon on the grass strip at the prison and taxied to the tie-down apron, where a prison correctional officer waited for us in a dark blue pickup truck. His military style clothing was also dark blue with red patches reading "LSP" (Louisiana State Penitentiary) on his sleeve, chest and baseball cap. On the way to the central trafficking building where the prisoner waited, Wellborn asked the correctional officer, "Anything exciting happen around here lately?"

"Yeah," he answered, "we had an escape attempt last week. Two trustees who worked up at the warden's house kidnapped the warden and his mother and tried to force him to drive them out of the prison." At the gate, the warden had crashed his car into a telephone pole, forcing the two men to attempt the rest of the escape on foot. The correctional officer went on to say that the response team had quickly cornered the two men against one of the prison's high double fences topped with razor ribbon. The prisoners were kneeling together against the fence with their hands clasped behind their heads when the warden arrived. Clearly distraught from the imminent danger in which the two had placed him and his mother, the warden took a rifle from one of the other correctional officers and shot the two men, killing the first and severing the other man's arm from his body.

I was shocked by this story. I was also troubled by the casual manner in which the correctional officer told us of the event. Judging by his matter-of-fact delivery, I assumed that the barbarity of this event was not unusual. The two men had simply gotten what they deserved, and no one could blame the warden for being upset and reacting the way he did.

I remained silent while we completed the brief journey to our destination at the prison, but I kept wondering to myself how many men were spending the remainder of their lives behind those fences for becoming "distraught," as the warden had, and killing someone.

I cannot say with certainty that Angola's warden has this blood on his hands, but years later I heard from several sources that there had been such an escape attempt, and the man who had lost his arm eventually testified in a court hearing that he and his partner had been hopelessly trapped between the fence and the armed band of correctional officers when the warden opened fire on them. However, the prisoner was not believed, and he was returned to Angola to spend the rest of his life there.

While Wellborn was in a private room interviewing his

witness, I waited in an area through which prisoners were routed to other areas of the prison. In the center of the room, there was a circular, glassed-in booth, not unlike the ticket booth of a theater. Inside sat a severely obese woman who was clearly in charge of the area. As prisoners arrived wearing shackles, she shouted out her orders and told them where to sit or stand. I noticed right away that no matter what any of them wanted to do, they first had to ask her permission. One prisoner who recognized an old friend asked the woman if he could speak to him. "You ain't gon' flirt w' yur girlfriend in here!" she responded. Another who was escorted in by a correctional officer and left standing had to ask her permission to sit down in one of the many open seats.

Within minutes, I realized that one would literally have to revert to the status of a child in order to mentally survive under this level of control. The longer I sat there, the more uncomfortable I became. Finally, unable to watch this any longer, I got up and walked outside.

There, I saw the work crews returning from the prison's cotton fields. Dressed in jeans, light-blue shirts and black knee-length rubber work boots, they marched in lines and carried hoes and shovels on their shoulders. The correctional officers, carrying high-powered carbines, accompanied them on horseback. As each prisoner turned in his tools, he was searched. Some were told to go into a small cinder block structure to be strip-searched. Nearly all of the prison correctional officers incessantly humiliated and goaded the prisoners and seemed unnecessarily cruel to them. As I witnessed all of this, I began to conclude that I would never be able to survive this kind of treatment without reverting to some kind of preadolescent stage of helplessness and rage. I would have to allow everything I had ever become as a man to die, and I knew that before I would permit that, I would simply kill myself or, perhaps, someone else.

As Wellborn and I flew away from the prison that afternoon, my thoughts were pervaded by a mixture of shock at what I had seen and fear at my own ignorance of the reality of such places. I felt as if there was a war zone less than one hour from my front door, but this war zone was an integral part of my own culture. I returned home a changed person. I had received the first wake-up call from my comfortable little world on the grassy Shreveport, Louisiana, hillside I called home.

My reaction, however, was not to march out and immediately begin to protest prison conditions, nor did I seriously consider changing my life in any way because of the experience. Why should I? I had been born poor and fought my way up out of poverty the hard way, and I was in no hurry to compromise my affluence and social position.

I could not forget what I'd seen, however. The unremitting

cruelty the correctional officers inflicted on the prisoners had stirred up an old and dark rage inside me. It took me back to a time when I'd been treated in a similar way during the summer of my sixteenth year, a week after my father had died. On the morning of my father's death, my brother told me I would have to find a "serious" summer job to help out at home—throwing newspapers and sacking groceries for my spending money would no longer be enough. A week later, I started work in a wholesale grocer business loading trucks in the morning and unloading boxcars in the afternoon. My father had worked his last years for a company that brokered its goods through this same warehouse, and my grandfather, who worked in the sales office of the warehouse, landed me the job. It was hard work and, of course, hot as hell.

What made the job truly miserable, though, was the warehouse boss. He resented me for getting the job and committed every cruelty I could imagine to get rid of me. I was too young and naïve to understand the purpose of his brutal attacks and, with no prospects for something better, I dared not defend myself.

The worst job was sliding open the boxcar doors to the most dreaded shipments of Paramount vinegars and pickles. Almost always, the switching of the railroad cars had shattered some of the gallon jars, mixing 150-degree heat with the choking fumes of evaporating vinegar. That smell, however, was still less overwhelming than my boss' incessant goading and his inestimable wrath.

I worked twelve hours a day, Monday through Saturday. The hours seemed so long that, by the end of my first day on the job, I felt as if I had been there an entire summer. I was only able to survive through the help of the black laborers in the warehouse, men who had known and deeply respected my father. Back then, such respect between races was branded as "nigger lovin'" by southern whites, and any white man who showed such feelings toward African-Americans was despised, insulted or slandered. This hostile attitude was reflected in some of the boss's more disgusting insults. "Yo daddy would fuck anything—race, color or creed." Even though I knew this was grossly untrue, I could not keep those words from searing through my body like exploding bullets. Furthermore, I soon realized that being my father's son made me guilty by association, which was probably the underlying explanation of the boss's merciless behavior towards me.

It's somewhat ironic, however, that these very relationships my father had with these laborers became one of his most vital legacies to me. Those men took me under their wings and taught me how to endure hard labor, how to shoulder the one hundred–pound flour sacks with my small frame and how to put up with the incessant insults that the boss threw at all of us. They told me what a fine man my father was and how much I looked like him and reminded them of him. They also encouraged me to remember that better days would come.

In spite of their encouragement, this sudden onslaught of daily misery and adversity, on top of the staggering grief I was carrying over the death of my father, left me feeling fairly wretched that summer of 1960. Gradually, however, I came to feel equally wretched for the black men who watched over me and who, for the most part, were stuck there forever. One day, I even tried organizing a strike in the name of better treatment, but they told me that they could not afford to risk their jobs and, instead, tried to console my growing rage. At the end of that first season, I swore to God and myself that I would never set foot in that place again. Nevertheless, I worked four more summers in that warehouse.

So it was that the death of my father had come to represent the death of my youth, its innocence and my sense that, even though I was poor, the world was a safe place. While my friends dreamed of carefree summers between the long semesters of high school, springtime signaled to me the return to cruel, humiliating days and bearing the sweltering heat of the boxcars at midday after the trucks had left to deliver their cases of canned goods and grocery stuffs.

As time went on, I developed a growing sense of horror that I might be stuck there for the rest of my life, a concern that was brought on by the fear that even if I managed to get into college, I would not make it through. Although a good education was my greatest dream, no one, with the exception of one uncle, in my family had attended college. However, the overriding reason I believed I would never make it was a statement I had accidentally seen on my performance report at the end of my freshman year in high school. My homeroom teacher had written, "Definitely not college material."

But attend college I did. Those dreaded summers, however, took their toll and led me to abandoning my earliest dreams of becoming a teacher or writer. Those dreams, I perceived, would not protect me from poverty and the ever-possible nightmare of winding up back in the warehouse or some place like it. Instead, I decided to try to become a dentist. As a dentist, I would never again have to put up with a boss of any kind; and the low self-image I had formed could be erased by the titles that accompanied the degree: doctor, professional, specialist, practitioner.

Notwithstanding the difficulties of those summers, the warehouse did serve to toughen me to the harshness and deceptions I would face in the adult world. Even though I had encountered the cruelest person I had ever met, I experienced the kindness of the black laborers and achieved a deeper understanding of the poverty and suffering of our culture's disenfranchised. Without question, those summers also prepared me to deal with the immeasurable cruelty I would encounter in the prisons and penitentiaries thirty years later, when I entered my second career.

I worked my way through dental school as a New Orleans cab driver and by the age of forty had achieved all of the material rewards that a poor boy in Louisiana could dream of earning. I had developed a successful practice in my hometown; I had a wife and four sons and a large house in the country with a pool; and I had lived in Europe. I held a position in local society and could afford expensive hobbies that reflected the rest of my lifestyle. For nine years, I raced sports cars in amateur events. Eventually, though, the excitement of racing diminished, even though I won almost every competition I entered. Flying, however, restored the excitement I craved, but I soon discovered that stunt flying, by comparison, could provide as great a rush as the first time I had sex.

In fact, it was the high risks of stunt flying that led me to yet another major wake-up call. I was once again flying in the annual Christmas air show in Natchitoches, Louisiana. My routine had not gone well, as I had devoted little time before the event to practicing. I had completely blown a maneuver known as an outside loop, and I became disoriented in the process.

I finished the performance just as I had planned, by pulling my Super Decathlon straight up toward the sky and holding on until it had almost completely run out of airspeed. If I had waited any longer, the plane would have stalled and begun falling into a tail slide. Since my plane was not designed to withstand the wind forces created by falling backwards, I kicked the left rudder pedal just before the stall and rotated 180 degrees so as to fall toward the ground headfirst. With this, I had executed what is known in stunt flying terms as a "hammerhead stall." As I rapidly gained speed, I abruptly pulled out of my headfirst fall about one hundred feet off the ground, well below the minimum altitude for which I was certified by the Federal Aviation Administration to perform in air shows. I nearly always ignored those minimums, figuring I was good enough, and I did not want to look amateurish, for I was performing with some well-known professional pilots. This time, as usual, I succeeded.

My grand finale always entailed passing in front of the crowd inverted, my wings wagging to their applause. This time, however, as I rolled inverted, the controls felt heavy—so much so that it was taking all my strength just to keep the nose from falling below the horizon—and the problem was rapidly getting worse. I had already placed my left hand over my right to push harder, and I did not dare take it off to readjust the trim control. I learned later that a screw that was supposed to provide friction on the trim lever had worked loose, and the lever could no longer hold the proper setting.

The nose of the plane was becoming heavier and heavier, and I knew that I must get it rolled upright. As I rotated the aircraft, my right wing came within inches of striking the ground and sending me into a cartwheeling crash. However, I landed safely, the entire sequence delighting the crowd.

Once I was on the ground, a friend rushed up to me to describe how close I had come to death. Though I never flew in another air show, I did not stop asking myself why I had spent the last twenty years driving like a maniac on the German autobahn, racing cars at tracks around the United States and stunt flying. It wasn't a shock to me that during the years I spent stunt flying, my marriage began to fall apart. As the stability of my life began to crumble, my search for excitement and stimulation slowly grew into a search for some kind of further purpose and meaning. While we were in marital therapy, my wife gave me a copy of Dr. M. Scott Peck's bestseller, *The Road Less Traveled*.

One day, while contemplating a compelling question about the nature of love, I called the author's office on a whim. To my surprise, Dr. Peck returned my call and, at the end of our forty-five minute discussion on love and marriage, I told him I would very much like to meet him someday and spend more time learning from him. "Well, I'm not very busy during the week of July Fourth. Why don't you come up for the week? We could have a session every day at my home, which is where I practice, and we'll see what happens. You can stay at an inn just down the road."

That week became one of the pivotal experiences of my life. At its end, Dr. Peck told me to return home, find a spiritual guide and continue my spiritual journey in earnest.

Not long after that fateful week, a friend told me about Dr. Spencer Murray, a Presbyterian minister who had left the pulpit to study psychology then returned to the church as a therapist to its parishioners. Since he was teaching a course on Dr. Peck's now-famous book, I was curious as to whether he might be the mentor Dr. Peck had told me to find. I approached the idea with some caution, as my goal was a spiritual journey and not a religious one.

Spencer was tall and thin with deep-set blue eyes that were focused and quick to smile. We met at four one Friday afternoon and spent the next two hours becoming acquainted. At the end of our conversation, he asked, "What do you want from me?" I told him I was seeking a spiritual guide and wondered if he was that person. He suggested that we both think about it and asked me to call him at the end of a week.

I did just that. "Well, what do you think?" he asked.

"I think I'd like to see you some more and find out where that leads us," I answered.

Spencer agreed. I made sure that he knew I was neither a member of his church nor even a Presbyterian. "That's all right," he replied. "When do you want to come in?"

I spent nearly two extraordinary years under Spencer's guidance. He taught me the practices of meditation and journaling, took me on silent retreats and convinced me to take some psychology courses at a local university. At times, during our weekly sessions, he would rear back in his chair laughing at my most serious and dreadful disclosures. I should have minded that, but I didn't. However, I became curious as to why I did not mind and asked him what he thought about it. He said, "Because deep down inside you know I'm not laughing at you—I'm laughing at myself for having done the same things in my own life and having been just as codependent."

I will always be grateful to Spencer for the time he devoted to me and especially for encouraging me to practice contemplative meditation. One of the most important experiences of my life occurred during one of my early morning meditative sessions. I had begun my practice at 4:30 that Saturday morning, long before any of my family was awake. About an hour had passed when suddenly I felt surrounded by a spirit whose presence felt so familiar that I thought it might be my soul. Emanating from it was the essence of unbounded love, as the spirit whispered a simple message, "I love you." This love was unlike any I had ever known or was perhaps something I had once lost and longed for all my life. Now, suddenly, it returned with such intensity that I wept unreservedly. Since that brief and blessed encounter, being somewhere on my own no longer meant loneliness, but merely solitude. For since that morning, I have never felt alone—lonely at times, but never alone.

At the same time of my life, I joined a training group of psychiatrists, psychologists and social workers who participated in group therapy as a way to hone their own techniques. The leader of that group, Douglas Greve, M.D., was a Gestalt therapy specialist and a tough instructor who consistently challenged our group with obstacles we had to overcome in order to accomplish our tasks.

It wasn't long before I found myself taking a full curriculum at the university, and I ultimately earned a master's in clinical social work. I became vastly intrigued by the human psyche and its capacity for healing. I soon became a noted specialist in the psychosomatics of a painful disorder of the jaw, TMJ, or temporomandibular joint pain dysfunction syndrome.

I also began my pursuit of a Ph.D. in curriculum and instruction, a course of study that allowed me to pursue my growing fascination with group psychodynamics. Dr. Peck, with whom I had kept in touch, was becoming a more powerful figure in my life, inviting me to train in the skills of leading large groups of people through a process he termed "community building." As much as I respected him, my experiences up to that point told me that he was probably way off base with this new idea. He was telling me that a group of fifty people could, in the span of a weekend, come to the level of deep sharing and cohesiveness that a typical therapy group of twelve (like my training group) normally takes three to six months to accomplish. In time, I agreed to attend a weekend community-building workshop that Dr. Peck's wife, Lilly, was leading in Winston-Salem, North Carolina.

I was surprised and moved by the sense of harmony and the level of intimacy fostered during that brief time. There were many people in the group who talked about their failures as parents. As the father of four sons, I related to their stories and spoke of my own failures as a father. When I talked about the apologies I was making to my sons, many wished that their parents were able to do the same to them or that their spouse was able to apologize to them or their children. These interactions were similar to the ones I had experienced previously in my training group, but something was different this time: The sharing of such intimacy and honesty with sixty-six people instead of twelve left me with a greater sense of release from the emotional burdens of my grief. My head felt less clouded without such emotions.

It also dawned on me that I was lonely. Though I had many friends, I did not know them and they did not know me on the level I experienced with my community members that weekend. To my friends and me, friendship mostly meant being polite. Getting angry with a friend would almost always mean an end to the relationship. The workshop, on the other hand, began in politeness and progressed into a long period of anger and conflict. Yet no one left.

Everyone came there with a commitment to hang together. As a result, we learned that we could disagree with each other without anyone being hurt, thus the anger did not drive anyone off. This made our circle a safe place to disclose what was underneath all the anger that weighed heavily on our hearts and minds. Perhaps my sense of loneliness was from not having friends at home with whom such honesty was possible.

The other important difference between that weekend and my friends was that, though the experience that weekend was very therapeutic, community building was not therapy. This meant that there was no one there to offer counsel or interpret hidden meaning in my grief. Since my head felt clearer, perhaps that sort of analysis was not necessary. Even though there was no one there to heal me, the experience was very healing. Finally, being real about myself with so many other people was a far cry from the social scene back home, and I definitely wanted more of this, which I would get.

Lilly Peck approached me following that weekend and asked if I had interest in training as a leader for future workshops. I quickly said yes and learned that, in order to qualify, I would be required to attend one more workshop as a participant. I immediately signed up for the next scheduled workshop, which was in two weeks.

There, I was introduced to Pat White, the CEO of Dr. Peck's new Foundation for Community Encouragement (FCE). Recognizing my skills in group process, she invited me to take part in a civilian diplomacy trip to the Soviet Union, where we would spend three weeks fostering community between one hundred Soviets and one hundred Americans. This was 1988, during the early days of *glasnost,* and the Russian people had just begun to internalize the freedoms of Mikhail Gorbachev's new policies of political and social openness. The community-building process work was done in groups of about twenty-five people, each group with a different theme. These themes ranged from my group on nationalism and stereotypes to groups working with addictions and others on art and music. Over a period of ten days aboard the cruise ship *Maxim Gorky,* we sailed down the Volga River from Kazan to the Black Sea, singing and dancing together every night. On some days, our groups took breaks to visit cities along the way and attend concerts in which our own musicians participated.

In spite of our differences in culture, politics and language, and a seventy-year history of cold warfare, we and our Soviet hosts bonded deeply and recovered the common denominators of shared humanity.

Soon after my return from the Soviet Union, I met with my Ph.D. committee at Louisiana State University (LSU) to discuss my dissertation. As I enthusiastically expounded the virtues of Dr. Peck's model and my experiences applying it in the Soviet Union, I asserted that it could be applied virtually anywhere. One of the professors challenged me by asking, "Could it work in a prison?"

Since I had been bragging with every superlative I could muster, I wanted to answer, "Why, of course." But, in fact, I hesitated—the idea had never even occurred to me.

I told the professor that I did not know the answer but could surely get it from Dr. Peck, whom I called that evening. His response was, "I don't know, Bob. But we'll never find out unless someone tries, and I wish *you'd* try."

I knew immediately that I would do just that, and for the next several weeks I thought a great deal about exactly how I would carry my efforts out. I imagined taking a weekend and putting on a community-building workshop at Angola, for instance. However, the professor who had asked about trying this model in a prison suggested that I try a more extensive investigation into the effects that the process would have on a prisoner's behavior, education and environment.

As I began to design the program and write the grant proposal, I felt my enthusiasm and a feeling of the "rightness" of this project growing exponentially. I felt compelled to continue, as if my soul was demanding that I do this.

So began the inner struggle between my soul's commands and my love of comfort and security. For the first time ever I found myself wanting to leave dentistry altogether. After a few weeks of hard reflection, I called the professor who had originally suggested the idea and told him that I was considering making this my life's work. He told me that for a long time he had been hoping I would say that.

Sadly, my already weakened marriage of twenty-four years could not withstand the radical changes that were occurring in my life. The relationship finally ended, as I announced my plans to sell my dental practice, office and instruments, and leave it all behind so I could conduct research in a prison. Everyone I knew—my family, my friends and my staff—was certain that I had completely lost my mind. I was not exactly spilling over with confidence that they were wrong, either. Still, I did not feel capable of interrupting the flow that had begun. When Governor Charles Roemer of Louisiana awarded me the grant I had proposed, I moved from my beloved family and pleasant hillside in the country to a small apartment in Baton Rouge and began my research, my dissertation and, indeed, my new life.

The Journey

One day you finally knew
what you had to do, and began,
though the voices around you
kept shouting
their bad advice--
though the whole house
began to tremble
and you felt the old tug
at your ankles.
"Mend my life!"
each voice cried.
But you didn't stop.
You knew what you had to do,
though the wind pried
with its stiff fingers
at the very foundations--
though their melancholy
was terrible.
It was already late
enough, and a wild night,
and the road full of fallen
branches and stones.
But little by little,
as you left their voices behind,
the stars began to burn
through the sheets of clouds,

and there was a new voice,

which you slowly

recognized as your own,

that kept you company

as you strode deeper and deeper

into the world,

determined to do

the only thing you could do--

determined to save

the only life you could save.

Mary Oliver

It wasn't long before another professor on my six-member committee, a man who had experience conducting research in prisons, offered me his assistance with some of the demographics of our prisons. He suggested that instead of going to Angola I begin at Dixon Correctional Institute (DCI), which is in Jackson, Louisiana. He was acquainted with the warden, Burl Cain, and he had established a friendly working relationship with him. DCI inhabitants, like 80 percent of all prisoners in the country, were male, medium-security prisoners. This meant that if we were successful at this prison, we could predict that the technique would work in most prisons in the country. Besides, DCI was considerably closer to my apartment in Baton Rouge.

Other demographics at DCI revealed that the prisoner population was 89 percent African-American, whereas the state's overall population was only 30 percent African-American. I did not concern myself at the time with the implications of these numbers, nor did I feel anxious about working mostly with black men. My Soviet experience had thoroughly convinced me that this process of community building could work anywhere. Besides, I had always felt at ease around African-Americans, given my experiences on the plantation where I had spent my early youth, and my days with those noble and nurturing black men with whom I had worked in the warehouse.

At an early age I became familiar with African-Americans' struggles with poverty. I had become aware that even though my family was poor, we were better off than the black families who lived in the shotgun shacks[†]—referred to by locals as the "nigger quarters"—on the plantation next to the muddy Bayou Pierre. Furthermore, though my mother, like my father, had to work every day to help us make ends meet, a white woman still drew a larger salary than a black woman. So it was that my mother could afford to hire a black woman to watch over her children after school and do some cleaning and cooking before she got home. For us, that woman was Parrie Boudry, and she

---

[†] A shotgun shack is a small, narrow house of three to four rooms. With all doors opened, one can see completely through it like the barrel of a shotgun.

became a second mother to me, a woman whom I have loved all my life.

These, though, were not the only reasons I grew up with the seeds of love and respect for African-Americans. Although segregation in that era was simply the way things were and the civil rights movement was unheard of at that time, my parents made certain that we understood that there should be respect among all people. As an example, I remember my father's relationship with the African-Americans on the farm, the way my father and them talked and laughed together, and how there was a mutual respect and camaraderie between them all. I also vividly recall how much those men *loved* him. My father must have understood on a very deep level what it was like to live as a minority in this country, perhaps because his mother, Tura, was half Cherokee Indian. I once heard that my Uncle Walter invited Tura to attend services at the Baptist church he had recently joined. She replied, "If God had wanted me in his house, he'd have given me lighter skin."

When my father was only five years old, Tura died. He was sent to live with his father's parents in Texarkana where they owned a small boardinghouse. Stories I have heard indicate that my dad's grandfather, Big Paw, was a brutal man who mistreated my father. Fortunately, an older black man named Joe, who worked for Big Paw, became my father's friend and protector. The measure of my father's love for this man is reflected in the fact that he eventually sought to carry Joe's name as his own. He began by refusing to respond to his given name, Jesse, and eventually made the change legally to the only name by which my father was known to me, Joe Earl Roberts.

I also remember Parrie's husband, Sunshine, sipping coffee in our kitchen one cold winter morning. He methodically poured his coffee into his saucer and blew on it before drinking. The Southern colloquialism, "all saucered and blowed," which refers to something that is standing by and ready to go, has always reminded me of Sunshine.

Finally, there was also the cold winter night when one of the shotgun shacks along the bayou caught on fire. Because the house was out in the country, there was no fire department to respond, nor was there even running water for a hose. Like their peers, the shack's inhabitants didn't keep their money in a bank, so all the money they had earned hoeing and picking cotton and saved for their kid's school clothes went up in flames. My mother, who had never before driven a truck, borrowed one from the farm the next morning. She drove into town and collected enough money, clothing and furniture for them to start over again.

On the whole, therefore, my upbringing left me somewhat confused when faced with the paradoxes of segregation in the old South. On the one hand, segregation was the "norm," yet I remained troubled by the intolerance and inhumanity born out of it. By the age of ten, for instance, I had accepted that blacks had to ride in the back of the trolleys, but one day when I looked toward the rear and saw my beloved Parrie sitting back there smiling at me as she always did, I was appalled.

Fortunately, as the years went by, the seeds of openmindedness and accountability that my parents had sown survived within me until the time when my spiritual journey led me downward into the Earth to shovel ashes from the smoldering fires of hatred and racism at Dixon Correctional Institute, in a circle of fifty angry men.

2

The Long Descent into Community

So there Rusty and I were, behind locked doors, in a circle with fifty male prisoners. As soon as our requested three minutes of silence were over, Billy, a prisoner who was sitting next to my colleague, Rusty, turned to him, got right in his face and demanded, "What the fuck you doin' here—you come here to fuck with our minds?" Billy was not much bigger than Rusty, but he was solid muscle. The expression on his face was serious and focused. "They payin' you to be here? How much they payin' you?" Wisely, Rusty carefully and calmly answered his questions with a brief "Yes," and, "Not much."

Then, Roland, another prisoner, told Billy to cool it. Roland, who stood about six feet, four inches, spoke with a deep voice and a centered authority. But his size and determination would not deter Billy. Hot words were exchanged between the two and, before we knew it, they were standing nose to chin in the middle of the circle, fists doubled. The only thing I knew for sure was that I should stay out of whatever was about to happen between them. I looked across the circle at Rusty, only to see one of the prisoners grab him so that he would not try to interfere between Billy and Roland. The prisoner's intention was to keep Rusty safe. Though my heart was racing, I did not move and could only hope I was not trembling. As suddenly as it had begun, however, the shouting ceased and the two men turned away from each other and took their seats. Later that day, one of the men said in private that he could not believe how cool I had been during the disturbance. Since we were not yet a community, I did not confess to him that I was anything but cool.

After Roland and Billy's confrontation, the men seemed to develop an attitude of curiosity about who we were and what our purpose for being there was. Soon, however, Rusty and I had gained enough confidence to stop answering their questions, saying respectfully that we did not feel moved to answer them. So, a roundtable discussion opened about the letter we had handed out the day before and about the guidelines for becoming a community, which we had read at the beginning of the day. The group tried to decipher hidden messages in our statements, and, in doing so, began to come together behind a common purpose.

It was not long before a leader emerged. He, too, attacked us verbally, but with more reason than aggression. He told all of us that he had been in prison for a long time and was not naive enough to think that the "system" was changing or that those who worked within it were about to do something to truly help him and the other prisoners. He wore typical prison clothing—blue jeans, a light-blue shirt and a jacket, with six-inch orange lettering that read "DCI" on all three pieces. He also had on a dark-blue stocking cap, pulled down over his ears. He kept his hands in his jacket pockets most of the time and his shoulders drawn up as if he were cold. He said his name was Malcolm.

I sensed a uniqueness about Malcolm, a certain "centeredness." His arguments were different from the others and were always addressed to the group. His assumptions were reasonable, based on his experiences, and on most accounts they were correct. We were not part of the prison system, so Malcolm was correct that the system was not offering help, nor was it changing. Although he still did not trust us, he seemed to have no desire to insult us, nor did he want to help us. He suggested that the group simply not cooperate with us because an attempt to do so would only give us grounds to report, as so many others had, that prison inmates were incapable of rehabilitation.

Then it dawned on him that, as long as he had to be there,

he could turn this into a forum for his own practical agenda. He began to request some behavioral changes in the dormitory. Respectfully, and skillfully, he asked the work crews that came in late at night to be a little more respectful of those who had to get up early the next morning. He asked everyone to be a little neater in the bathrooms by washing out the sinks after shaving. He stated that he understood everyone was pissed off at the system, but leaving the lavatories dirty only made more work for other prisoners, not the system. "Things could be just a little less miserable for all of us here if we would cooperate with each other a little."

Initially, no one responded to his suggestions, even though they were good ones. It was still very early in the "life" of the group and, as such, the group was yet incapable of functioning cooperatively or even considering it.

At lunchtime, as is the custom in community building, Rusty and I accompanied the group to eat. Arrangements had been made for the group to eat separately from the rest of the prison population. As my tray was filled with my first prison food, I turned to find that the only place left to sit was right in the middle of everyone. As I ate, my uneasiness faded and I felt entirely safe.

The afternoon session was filled with preaching and empty words. Many of the men had voluntarily and/or involuntarily gone through drug treatment programs while incarcerated that were predominantly inadequate. It's unfortunate that in these programs they learned only to proselytize the jargon and slogans of recovery: "I just gotta stop my stinkin' thinking," and "I'm sick and tired of bein' sick and tired." These clichés lacked substance and meaning and led us through a long period of boredom and agony that lasted the remainder of the day. However, this behavior was typical for most groups at this stage of community building, and it continued through the next morning until about ten, when the group shifted into conflict.

—⸺—

Better than anyone, Michael Meade, the well-known mythologist and storyteller, has characterized the difficult journey to becoming a community.

> *If the First Layer of human interaction is the common ground of manners, kind speech, polite greeting and working agreements; if the Third Layer is the area of deeply shared humanity, the universal brotherhood and sisterhood of all people, of the underlying, fundamental oneness of human love, justice and peaceful coexistence; then the Second Layer is the territory of anger, hatred, wrath, rage, outrage, jealousy, envy, contempt, disgust and acrimony. It is the* Via Negativa, *the field of Conflict, the plain of Discord, the hills of Turmoil. And the*

Second Layer always exists between the First Layer and the Third.

Cultures that try to shut out the Second Layer wind up with overcrowded prisons, high crime rates, huge black markets and, finally, riots in the streets. There's more bad news. The only way out of the First Layer, the only way to break the spell of niceness when it has shifted from ensuring life's continuance to insulting life's purpose is to enter the turmoil of the Second Layer. Furthermore, the only way to find the next location of the Third Layer is by traversing the battle-scarred, dog-infested terrain of the Second Layer.

Conflict among men always has the potential to become violent, and men in prison perhaps understand this better than most. For many in our group, in particular for the older men, the conflicts of the Second Layer were somewhat disturbing. As the level of chaos deepened, therefore, the group developed strategies to slip back and forth between the boring mixture of politeness and pseudocommunity (the First Layer) and chaos (the Second Layer).

The wide age range among the men brought about a corresponding diversity of attitude and behaviors. It was no surprise that the younger members were rebellious, snickering and taunting. I was impressed, however, by the genuine concern and caring that the older prisoners showed toward the youngsters. The older men, who had learned how to do their

time in prison and survive the brutalities of both other prisoners and the correctional officers, began to reach out and
caution the young men about the perilous circumstances they
were facing and of which they were often unaware.

One of these older men, James McGhee, was a short, stocky
individual who, because of his small size, had spent his spare
time during his many years in prison lifting weights. James had
developed himself into the perfect physical specimen of a man
not to be messed with. Recently, he had seen some of the
young men in the group annoying an older prisoner whose reputation for violence was well known to him. "You don't fuck
around with this dude, man," James warned. "I seen him kill a
dude at Angola 'cause the dude kept walkin' too close to his
bunk. Man, you gotta learn how to do yo' time or you ain't gon'
make it outta here. I seen some of you sitting on the toilet with
both feet in yo' pants. Man, you don't sit like that in prison.
Some dude pissed off at you see you like that, he'll kill you, man.
How you gon' fight some dude with both feet in yo' pants?"

Some of the stories the older men shared with the younger
ones were horrifying. There were stories of men stabbed to
death, burned to death, beaten to death, as well as tales of
heads cut off or split open and brains spilled out onto the
ground. Malcolm told the group that the only advice he had
gotten on his first day at Angola was to either get tough or
find a husband. Some who tried to get tough lost their lives in
the process.

Wilbert Rideau, a prisoner of forty years at Angola, described one such story in his book, *Life Sentences*.

A nineteen-year-old named Dunn was admitted to Angola in March of 1960 to serve a three-year sentence for burglary. A month after he got there, he received a call to go to the library. Once there, another prisoner shoved him into a dark room where two others waited in ambush. A thundering blow to his head rendered the boy helpless as the three men repeatedly raped him. "When they finished, they told me that I was for them, and then went out and told everyone else that they had claimed me." Terrified, all Dunn could think about was wanting to survive. He knew that once the men had "claimed" him, there was nothing he could do, short of killing one of them. Knowing he had only a three-year sentence, and wanting desperately to go home, Dunn decided to "try to make the best of it." An incident that he witnessed greatly influenced his decision: "During my first week here, I saw fourteen guys rape one youngster 'cause he refused to submit. They snatched him up, took him into the TV room and, man, they did everything to him—I mean everything. . . . When they finished with him, he had to be taken to the hospital where they had to sew him back up; then they had to take him to the nuthouse at Jackson 'cause he cracked up." Shaking his head at the memory, Dunn says: "Man, I didn't want none of that kind of action, and my only protection was in sticking with my old man, the guy who raped me."

WILBERT RIDEAU & RON WIKBERG, LIFE SENTENCES (TIME BOOKS, 1992)

Rideau added a chilling point when he said, "Few female rape victims in society must repay their rapists for the violence he inflicted upon them by devoting their existence to servicing his every need for years after—but rape victims in the world of prison must." Dunn, like many others before him, became his rapist's "old lady," his "wife."

Although I had fully expected to hear terrible stories during this workshop, I was horrified by what I was learning. I had always heard that rape and violence were part of prison life, but I had not thought a lot about it. Moreover, besides my shock at learning about the level of violence in all its horrifying details, I felt shame that I had ever laughed at the jokes I'd heard about prisoners being raped. I was ashamed of my lifelong narrow-mindedness and my unwillingness to overcome my ignorance about the realities of what goes on in prisons. I felt ashamed that I had bought into that segment of society that says, "Well, they deserve it." Now I thought, *No one deserves this*.

After several stories of prison rape, one of the older men brought up the sensitive subject of manhood, or what it means to be a man. The topic brought on an immediate reaction from the group, in particular from the younger members, most of whom became verbally defensive. "I got no problem bein' a man. I don't need to be in here [in this meeting] if that's what we gon' do," they vehemently affirmed.

I learned quickly that even raising the question of manhood to the young prisoners was interpreted as a threat to their safety, since they were the ones who were raped in prison. It was important for each to say, in so many words, "Don't fuck with me. Before you 'turn me out,' you will have to kill me first." In prison, an individual is one of two things: a man or a whore.

———

At that point, Joe Stanley spoke up for the first time. At sixty-four, Joe was probably the oldest person in the group. Standing six and a half feet tall, with salt-and-pepper hair, he had a mustache, goatee and the largest feet that I had ever seen. Joe had foot problems and walked with a slight limp. Major Price, a unit commander at the prison, had introduced me to Joe and told me in Joe's presence that I had better watch out for him. "He's a con man. You sit down and talk with him and, before you know it, he'll have your wallet."

What a lousy thing to say right in front of someone, I thought. *Even if it's true.* Besides, how much more difficult is it for a person to change when there's no one in his corner and no one who expects him to? Joe had tried to disguise his embarrassment with a slight smile, but his sad eyes and wrinkled brow gave him away.

Since we met, I got to know a bit more about Joe. His reading score on the test we had given the prisoners was one of the two highest among all three dorms, higher than I usually scored on such tests. However, at this point Joe had neither a diploma nor a GED certificate, though eventually he decided to take the GED exam and passed it with no classes or any other type of formal preparation. A handsome man with great clarity of speech, Joe filled his spare time by reading, and I noticed that he always brought some kind of book with him.

"Let me read you something about being a man," Joe said to the group as he looked through the pages of a book of poetry he had brought to the workshop. Joe began to read Rudyard Kipling's poem "If."

> If you can keep your head when all about you
> Are losing theirs and blaming it on you;
> If you can trust yourself when all men doubt you,
> But make allowance for their doubting too;
> If you can wait and not be tired by waiting,
> Or being lied about, don't deal in lies;
> Or being hated, don't give way to hating,
> And yet don't look too good, nor talk too wise;
>
> If you can dream—and not make dreams your master;
> If you can think—and not make thoughts your aim,
> If you can meet with Triumph and Disaster
> And treat those two impostors just the same;
> If you can bear to hear the truth you've spoken

Twisted by knaves to make a trap for fools,
Or watch the things you gave your life to, broken,
And stoop and build 'em up with worn-out tools;

If you can make one heap of all your winnings
And risk it on one turn of pitch-and-toss;
And lose, and start again at your beginnings
And never breathe a word about your loss;
If you can force your heart and nerve and sinew
To serve your turn long after they are gone;
And so hold on when there is nothing in you
Except the Will which says to them: "Hold on!"

If you can talk with crowds and keep your virtue
Or walk with kings—nor lose the common touch,
If neither foes nor loving friends can hurt you,
If all men count with you, but none too much;
If you can fill the unforgiving minute
With sixty seconds' worth of distance run,
Yours is the Earth and everything that's in it,
And—which is more—you'll be a Man, my son!

Complete silence hung in the room. As Joe continued to
stare at the book, perhaps himself contemplating the meaning
of what he had just read, I began to imagine what potential
these older men held as mentors and elders for the younger

ones. Slowly, questions arose in my mind. Why couldn't prisons be more like *this?* Prisons, I realized, have enormous potential to be places where men learn the responsibilities of manhood and learn respect for themselves and others. Instead, these guys were not allowed to be responsible for anything. They were told when to sleep, when to get up, when to eat, when to work, when to get a haircut and even when to go to the bathroom.

Furthermore, I could see that the very demography and architecture of this prison represented the antithesis of what society aims for when it speaks of "rehabilitation." No one would ever define rehabilitation as "leaving prison knowing how to play pool and watch television." Yet, at DCI, after a man had spent his day laboring at a fruitless job, the most accessible areas in the prison units were the recreation rooms, where one would only find a television set and a few pool tables.

If a prisoner wanted to attend an Alcoholics Anonymous or a Narcotics Anonymous meeting, a correspondence course or a rehabilitation program, he needed to arrange permission days in advance. After a long day of hard labor, he had to shower, change clothes, receive permission to leave and walk outside to the sally port, the double-gated checkpoint devised in medieval times for castles and walled cities. There he would often be made to stand in the open for forty-five minutes or more—possibly in extreme heat, cold or rain—waiting to attend a two-hour class or meeting. On the way through the sally port, he would be searched, perhaps strip-searched, and most likely humiliated in some way. Many times over the years of our study, my team and I waited in an empty room for the first hour of a scheduled two-hour class period because of such delays at the sally port, which was, among other things, a waste of the federal tax dollars we were paid to conduct our research. To make matters worse for the prisoners, because the area where classes and rehabilitation programs are held is close to the crawfish and onion plant at DCI, often those who tried to make it to a program or class became convenient targets and were pressed into duty on the night shift when the correctional officers were shorthanded at the plant.

Once classes were over, the rule at DCI was that the men had to be escorted back to their dormitories. Very often, this meant that they would be herded in the opposite direction to another area called The Bullpen, where they would sometimes be forced to stand and wait from nine at night until midnight, or even two in the morning, for a correctional officer to escort them to their dorm. Since the next morning began at five, this treatment was hardly incentive for self-improvement. Meanwhile, dormmates spent their evening playing pool, watching television and getting to bed early.

A university professor of political science who donated his time to help the men with their courses told me a story about monitoring a dozen prisoners who were taking final exams for a correspondence course. Soon after the men had begun their exams, two correctional officers walked in, tapped five of them on the shoulder, and said, "You, go pick crawfish."

Soon after our research project got underway, I met with the warden about losing men from my *own* classes. The warden explained that Prison Enterprises produced a significant portion of the corrections department's budget for the state. Therefore, the state had become heavily dependent on the labor of its prisoners. That is why states like Louisiana do not spend tax dollars on rehabilitation—they cannot afford to give their prisoners the time to attend such programs.[2]

—⸫⸫—

By mid-afternoon on the second day of the two-and-a-half-day workshop, the group still seemed hopelessly locked in chaos and conflict, and the preaching and philosophical nonsense seemed to go on forever. About half of the group seemed to have either "checked out" or fallen asleep. I had experienced discouragement with other groups, of course, but my feelings at this point bordered on despair. One of the more enduring orators, Harris, was presenting another of his sermonettes, pontificating about whose fault it was or wasn't that they were all in prison. The men were barely paying attention to him and no one was even interested enough to confront the futility of what he was saying.

"None of this is our parents' fault," lectured Harris. "People try to blame their parents. They didn't put us in here. We put ourselves in here. We took the drugs and we sold the drugs, and we got no one to blame 'cept ourselves. You do da' crime, you gotta do da' time."

Suddenly, Eric spoke up. Eric's nickname was Catfish; his eyes protruded somewhat and one of them was walleyed, giving him the appearance of looking in two directions at once. His white skin was rough and wrinkled beyond his relatively young age, and his receding hair was long and scraggly. Until this moment, he had been silent throughout the workshop.

"You know, for my part, I agree with you," he said. "I did take those drugs myself. And I sold drugs to get more drugs, and that's how I got caught and wound up in here. But, let me tell you something," he said, glaring sharply at Harris. "When I was a kid, my father used to beat me so hard with a water hose I couldn't go to school sometimes for a week. There were times, I think, I should'a been in the hospital. You know, the first thing I remember learnin' about survival in my life was that, when the leaves started fallin' off the trees in the fall, I needed to get a blanket and hide it in the dog house, because my dad would come home drunk at night and, if he got pissed off at me, he'd go out and cut a piece of that water hose and beat me with it. And that hose was *so* hard in the winter."

As he said this, Eric rolled his head back and across his shoulders, as if feeling the pain of those beatings all over again. "Then he'd throw me out of the house, and I'd be left out there till he passed out and my mother would let me back in. But, until then, I needed that blanket in the dog house to keep me from freezing."

Still looking at Harris, his eyes a bit redder now and slightly moistened, Eric said, "Yeah, like you say, I sold those drugs, and I took 'em, an' I don't blame anybody but myself. But, somehow, I think what my dad did to me had *something* to do with my bein' here."

With Eric's story, the atmosphere of the room began to shift. I wondered if the long descent into community was about to begin. I'd seen it in groups before. Rusty and I waited to see how the group would respond, if it did at all, to Eric's story. There was a minute or two of silence, then . . .

"My name is Fred. My dad was a pitcher for the Philadelphia Phillies. He was the only one from our town to ever play professional sports, and he was the town hero. But, the first thing *I* remember learning about survival was that I could recognize the squeal of the brakes on his truck from a block away. I'd run out the door and leave my mother to be the one who got beat up, and I always felt ashamed of that. There were several times he beat me or my mom up so bad, she'd call the sheriff. But the sheriff of our parish and my dad grew up together, and they were best friends. He'd tell my dad to calm down and not beat on us any more.

"But it kept happening till finally one day I heard him tell my mom he was gonna kill her. And the way he was hitting her, I really thought he was gonna do it. I thought, *I just gotta stop this once and for all,* so I grabbed the shotgun and killed him. And the people in our town were angry at me. I'd killed their goddamn hero."

Fred paused to get control of his voice. "Goddammit, I was gonna make it out of all that. I was in high school, president of my class, and I had a four-point average. But I been in and out of prison ever since.

"My little boy came to see me last Saturday. On the way back to my dorm, he spotted me through the fence and waved and said, 'I love you, Daddy.' I said, 'I love you too, son.' About that time, fuckin' Sergeant Bergeron yelled loud as he could, 'Git yo' ass down dat walk, Patterson, an' quit talkin' t'ru' dat fence.' I'll never forget the look on my little boy's face. I don't even feel human in here anymore." Another few moments passed in silence.

"My name is Andrew," said a big, handsome, soft-spoken man in his early twenties who had somehow earned the nickname of Psycho. "My father is a minister, but the thing I remember most about him and my mother was the way they use ta fight. When I was about five or six, I don't know, they was yellin' an' screamin' an' trying to kill each other. My father was holding my mother down on the floor, hittin' her, and she was screamin' and kickin' him. Both of them started yellin' at me to go get the kitchen knife. I was scared. I wouldn't go get it 'cause I didn't know which one to give it to. I just kept cryin' and screamin' at them to stop."[†]

I began to feel the group finally coming together, becoming bound by the common thread of their profound grief. I recalled what Robert Bly, the renowned poet/activist, had once taught me—that people grow close together into mean-ingful relationships not by sharing their victories, but through sharing their failures; not through talking about the ways in which they have it all together, but through talking about the ways in which they are broken apart; and not about the ways in which they have healed, but the ways in which they have been wounded.

The men's stories continued. Another member of the group spoke about the man who had moved in with his mother when he was little. "He wouldn't let my mother feed me and my brother. He said we weren't his an' so we couldn't eat his food. My mother would sneak us through the back door into the kitchen while he was in the living room readin' the paper. She would feed us out of the cookin' spoon right off the stove. Sometime after that, she gave us to my grandmother. She [grandmother] didn't want us, so she gave me to my uncle. He

---

[†] The by-products of children witnessing such violence are profound. Empirical studies have demonstrated consistently that when a child has been exposed early in his life to episodes of physical violence, *regardless of whether he himself is the victim or the witness*, he will often later demonstrate similar outbursts of uncontrollable rage and violence of his own.

didn't want me either, so I just left. I been on the streets since I was nine years old." Silence.

"My name is Bubba, an' I'm tryin', but I just can't do this, you know. I wanna say somethin', but I just can't start talkin' about myself like this."

Here it comes, I thought. I had seen this happen in groups many times before: Someone would declare his or her refusal or inability to open up like this and then would take the group down to its deepest level yet.

Bubba Sanders, one of only four white men in the group, said, "My family doesn't even come to see me—only one that ever did was my sister, and that was only once. I was in the hole that weekend for being late for work, not even a violent offense. And they brought me out to see her in chains from my neck to my feet. They didn't have to do that. Anyway, when my sister saw me that way, she was horrified. She cried an' cried, and said she couldn't stand to see me that way. An' she never came back."

Gary Benoit, who became a self-taught, certified paralegal while serving a sentence at Angola for manufacturing methamphetamine, told a similar story about being placed in full shackles and informed that both of his parents had just been killed in an auto accident in North Carolina. "It was the first time I remember hearing the term 'ol' thang,'" Gary said. "Two guards drove out in a pickup truck to the field where I was workin' and said, 'C'meer ol' thang.' They shackled me up without a word, put me in the back of the truck and drove off. The chaplain didn't ask them to take the shackles off me while he told me what had happened, so I even had to pray with 'em on. Then they drove me to the cell block (isolation) and kept me there alone for three weeks."[†]

As Gary spoke of the intense hatred he had for the correctional officers who waged a ceaseless psychological warfare against the prisoners, my attention intensified. His accounts of not being able to defend himself against humiliation and cruelty pierced my chest and made my heart pound, and I began to recall those days in the warehouse following the death of my father. Suddenly and vividly, the humiliation and shame I felt from the boss' persistent attacks came back. And Gary was talking about living every day under a far worse kind of tyranny.

"My name is Bob," I said, looking over at Gary. "I think I can understand, on some level at least, what you're talking about. Four days after my father died when I was sixteen, I went to work in a warehouse where . . ." As I spoke, I became aware of my own grief. Tears; my throat tightened; my voice hoarse.

"So when I hear the correctional officers talk to one of you

[†] As far as I have been able to determine, "Ol' thang" is a colloquial term unique to the security personnel at Angola. It is another example of the dehumanizing way that prisoners are addressed. Sometimes I've wondered if using a number to refer to the men wouldn't be better.

like that, there's a place in me that hurts terribly for myself and for you also." I wept for them all, then silence.

After a few moments, James McGhee slowly leaned forward from his seat, resting his hand on his knee with his elbow raised up so that the huge muscles of his arm stood out. He cocked his head to the side, looked down for a moment, then looked around at everyone in the group, "You know," he said, glancing over at me, "he care." Silence.

"My name is Bubba." *Here we go again,* I thought. "There's something I didn't say before. You know, I just turned twenty-four an' I been incarcerated for thirteen of those years. Been down so much of my life, the outside world for me is just a dream. My family put me in an institution the first time when I was six because they said they couldn't handle me. That Christmas was the year I learned there was no such thing as Santa Claus, when one of the older boys told me. I was so sad and remember thinking I was too young to have been told that then.

"Anyway, at that place they beat me up a lot. It got so bad that one day, when I was nine, I escaped. When the Mississippi State Police found me several days later, they said I had walked seventy-five miles north on a railroad track. I remember them takin' pictures of my legs 'cause they were so bruised from the beatings.

"The state police wouldn't turn me back over to the institution. They told my parents they had to come get me or they would just keep me in Mississippi an' put me somewhere. So my parents came an' got me. After that, my dad had to move us out of the country to Colombia 'cause my mother had built up $37,000 of debt on her credit cards. That was where I first got hooked on cocaine. I smuggled some back with me when we returned a couple of years later. My dad beat me when he found out 'cause of the trouble I could'a got him into, an' he broke my arm."

As the stories continued to surface, I could feel the group going further and further down, as if into the deep and dark "well of grief" described so well by poet David Whyte in his poem by that name.

The Well of Grief

Those who will not slip beneath
 the still surface on the well of grief

turning downward through its black water
 to the place we cannot breath

will never know the source from which we drink,
 the secret water, cold and clear,

nor find in the darkness glimmering
 the small round coins
  thrown away by those who wished for something else.

Whenever I speak of my first experiences with community building in prison, many people ask, "Were you being conned?" My answer is a clear and simple, "No." What I heard cannot be faked or acted out. When stories get this real, no one in the room can mistake them for lies. The men of Dorm 7 were not bragging about their toughness. They were not complaining or seeking pity. They were people unloading burdens they had carried for years, burdens that had weighed them down with guilt, shame, rage and grief because there had been no place to lay them. They had no one to listen to them, no container that could hold their anguish, no environment safe enough to let them be heard.

During one of these stories, I looked over at Renaldo, a scraggly bearded Colombian national in prison for smuggling cocaine into the United States. Though he spoke no English, his face and his eyes were as alert as anyone else's in the room. A deaf man could have recognized the realness of the group just by looking at the faces and their eyes, tears and grief that filled the room.

At one point during these stories, Malcolm spoke up and apologized for the things he had said the day before. "Yesterday, when I said that I didn't believe you guys had anything good to offer us, I didn't understand what you were really doin'. I was wrong. I can see now, by what is happenin' in this room, and by the fact that Bob actually cried tears for our pain and told us how much he hurt when his father died, that you guys are different. I'm thinkin' maybe this program does have something good to offer us."

Malcolm was not the only one. By the end of the day, many of the men had apologized, both publicly and privately, for their negative attitudes and all the jive and harassment they had subjected us to in the beginning. Another participant who, on the first day, had stood up from his chair to shout that he did not trust me and that I had better not ever trust him, got up out of his seat, crossed the circle and gave me a hug. I don't remember why, but at that moment I happened to look at my watch. I noticed that this drastic transformation had somehow occurred over a time span of only twenty-two hours.

Some of the men began to talk about the sense of relief they felt after telling their stories. Others spoke of more subtle things. I overheard one participant say to another, "I've lived in the bunk next to you for four years and I didn't know your name was Steve."

Another said that when he got back to the dorm that evening, he was going to call his father, whom he had talked about that day, and tell him for the first time that he loved him.

The greatest surprise of the day, though, came when several men admitted that they "couldn't read a lick," and asked the group, "Will someone please teach me to read?"

I realized that, already, my most important questions had been answered. "Could prisoners build community together?" Yes, they could. And without this answer, we would have been able to go no further. The future of the entire study rested on whether or not these men could overcome the hardened codes of prison culture to unload their darkest secrets in a room full of other prisoners, where there were no guarantees against exploitation or even a guarantee of confidentiality. Would they be capable of crossing the field of conflict without shedding blood? Could they refrain from the violence long enough to get down underneath their rage and talk about the shame that, for a lifetime, they had covered up with toughness and numbed with drugs? The answer was yes.

Now, to our great joy and relief, we could begin the next step. We could find out if such a community could be maintained within a prison culture. We could learn what effects, if any, their community-building experiences would have on their ability to improve their education, reduce violence within the walls of the prison and perhaps find a more decent way of survival, whether inside prison or out. It was clear that some deep transformations had taken place, but what was not clear was whether the greatest transformations had taken place in them or in me.

CHAPTER
3

Malcolm

*I*t had taken a day and a half of chaos, angry complaining and pontificating before the men could begin to remove some of their armor, let go of some of their prejudices and preconceptions and, in the process, become a community. As the two-and-a-half-day workshop came to a close, Rusty and I met to debrief and discuss the next stage of the seven-week program I had designed for the research study: the literacy training workshops.

We had both come to the conclusion that Malcolm Hill, who had so fervently opposed our effort in the beginning, should become one of the participants that we would train as a community-building leader. Malcolm was someone whom

other prisoners *and* even security personnel regarded as a natural leader, a peacemaker and a skilled arbitrator of disputes.
Because of these qualities, the Muslim community at the prison
had made him their Imam (ee-MAHM)—their spiritual
leader—even though he was not a Muslim. And, because of the
respect that security personnel held for him, Malcolm was able
to move about the prison more freely than the other prisoners,
a privilege that would be of great help to us as time went on.

After clearing our choice for a community-building leader
with the warden, Rusty and I went over to Dorm 7 to discuss
the idea with Malcolm. So as not to arouse jealousy among
the other prisoners, the conversation needed to be private,
and Major Price, the unit commander, allowed us to meet
with Malcolm in a front office.

Malcolm had a shaken look on his face as he entered the
room, as such callouts often meant trouble with security or a
death in the family. Malcolm relaxed, however, when he saw
our smiles. He was deeply moved when I told him why we had
asked him to come. "I had been wonderin' what God had in
store for me next," he admitted. "I'm honored to be joinin'
with y'all in this effort of helpin' the men here."

—————

As planned, the next seven weeks were filled with reading classes for both Dorm 7, the treatment group, and Dorm

A, the control group that was participating in the reading program without first becoming a community. In the reading sessions, Rusty and I split the two larger groups into smaller ones based on the various reading abilities. Those who could read well were mixed with average, below-average readers and nonreaders. Their only instructions were to use the material provided to help each other learn to read better. Classes met three times a week for two hours.

Of course, the differences between the way that the men of Dorm 7 and the men of Dorm A responded to this directive to work together were immense. The men of Dorm 7 went right to work. Those who could not read had already talked openly about it in the community-building sessions, even sharing stories about the shame they had experienced when, at a young age, they were labeled as slow, ungifted or a failure.

As Rusty and I observed the accomplished readers, we were amazed to see how these men, whom society thought of as tough misfits and rejects, instantly became teachers who were willing to work patiently with the other men and give them basic reading instruction. We believed in the old adage, "No one learns more than the teacher." Therefore, we also believed the reading skills of the men who were willing to take on the job of instructor would also increase, and their levels of self-esteem would rise as they discovered their ability to help someone who needed them.

The self-esteem of the nonreaders and the low-level readers

soon rose as their skills steadily improved and they received praise from their teachers. This was extra gratifying since the reading experts at LSU had warned us not to get our hopes up about the success of our literacy program goals. We would be working with men who they believed would require specially trained remedial reading instructors in order to learn anything. These experts were amazed, to say the least, when they saw the post-test reading scores of Dorm 7 and discovered that, as a group, the dorm's reading skills had averaged an increase of one grade level in the short seven-week period.

The reading group from Dorm A was much less communicative and cooperative, although a few men obviously wanted to take advantage of any opportunity that would upgrade their education. Among this group of prisoners was a trained literacy instructor, Larry Brown, who made concerted efforts to help the others. Unfortunately, his efforts were accepted on a very limited basis. The deep levels of trust and effective communication that had become so characteristic of the Dorm 7 group were simply not available to the men of Dorm A. The only difference between these two groups was that one was a community, the other was not.

During the weeks and months that followed, my relationship with Malcolm deepened into a true friendship as we told our stories to each other and to the participants of Dorm 7's ongoing community-building sessions. We were not surprised by the dissimilarities in our lives, but at times we were amazed by the amount of very similar experiences we shared. Malcolm had also spent his earlier (and happier) years on a farm, and his family was also poor. By the age of nine, however, we had both moved to urban areas and were leading lives that were headed in different directions—one towards success as society defines it and the other towards a life of crime, drugs and prison.

In our young-adult years, we both pursued dangerous lifestyles, one legal, the other illegal, but both inevitably damaging. While I was racing cars, Malcolm was stealing them. As Malcolm was getting high on heroin in New York, I was getting high on my own adrenaline rush from stunt flying, an addiction not much less dangerous and destructive to my family than the use of illicit drugs.

With our lives in chaos, we had both begun to make transformations with the guidance of mentors at about the same time. Malcolm's mentor was a gray-haired old man he met at Angola, Leonard Johnson, who had taken on the Muslim name of Mwalemu, which means "teacher." A militant protester from the sixties, he had reputedly been a modern-day Robin Hood who robbed banks and gave the money to the poor. Wounded in a shootout with FBI agents on Canal Street in New Orleans, he was paralyzed from the waist down and sentenced to life imprisonment. He told Malcolm one day that, in spite of Malcolm's hatred for whites, Malcolm would meet a white man who would become his closest ally and friend.

Now, as Malcolm and I both made radical changes in our lives and began the work of healing the wounds to our own souls, our two paths had crossed behind the prison walls at DCI, and we were beginning a new journey together. Though we were serving a higher purpose, our difficulties would soon increase, but so would our fulfillment and joy.

Much of that fulfillment and joy came in the form of the long evening conversations we shared on days when I could stay on after the dormitories were shut down for the night. During this time, most of the other men were checked out, listening to a Walkman, sleeping, reading or watching television.

"At the age of nine," Malcolm told me on one such evening, "my parents moved from the farm we lived on into the city limits. That was a major turning point in my life, as I became aware of color for the first time. That was also where, for the first time, I saw my father become drunk and violent with my mother. I saw my whole family coming apart as I experienced what it was like to not have enough—enough food, toys, attention, love and caring from my parents. There always seemed to be less of everything we had when we left that farm."

Malcolm's parents had been sharecroppers living a simple life when they lost their farm. So, at a very young age Malcolm knew that his family was very, very poor. "Because I saw it in my mother's eyes," he told me. "I saw it in my father's eyes. They struggled to always put a meal on the table." Malcolm remembered that when he was eleven or twelve he would go to the refrigerator and only see a container of water. He knew he had to do something to help. "I didn't understand it because my father and mother were working every day. So one day I went to a supermarket and I shoplifted some food. I'll never forget, it was a pack of steak and a pound of rice, not enough to feed the family, because I come from a very large family of thirteen, but I knew it was something. And my mother looked at me, and she told me, 'You can't bring that in here, because you didn't pay for it.'

"That hurt me then and still hurts today, because I didn't see anything wrong with people trying to feed themselves. I saw something wrong with a supermarket with a lot of food in it, and here you got a family with nothing to eat. I still see something wrong in that."

There was another time when Malcolm tried to help his family. He and his father had ridden to the home of a man for whom his father had worked a couple of weeks driving trucks. When they arrived, the man wouldn't pay him. It was near Christmas, and the man told Malcolm's father he didn't have the money. "I got so furious and upset, I really wanted to hurt him. I wanted to do something," Malcolm remembered, "but when I got out of the truck and was about to approach the man to tell him something, my father stopped me. He yelled at me and threatened to whip me, and told me he'd never take me anywhere with him again. I'm sitting there looking at this white man, big old fine home and all these trucks he had, and he's telling my father he doesn't have the money to pay him. I just wanted to protect my father. I felt like I wanted to get what belonged to him. I couldn't just watch all this going on and not do nothing."

I could feel the emotion stirring in him as he talked about those times. "It didn't have to be like that," he said. And there was no doubt in his mind that watching his family suffer had contributed to the lifestyle of vice, crime and drugs in which he eventually became involved. "But my initial purpose for getting involved in criminal activity was to try to relieve some of the pressure on my parents, to try and provide a better life for my family."

Malcolm's efforts to help his family eventually lead to numerous brushes with the law. And the more he succeeded in getting away with breaking the law, the better he began to feel about himself. "I felt like it was a great accomplishment. I was able to lie down at night and know within my heart that I was able to do something well and had succeeded at doing it. I guess I got away too many times because it never stopped. I kept on and on and on."

Malcolm told me that his father never would come to the jail to bail him out when he got arrested, and he would tell Malcolm's mother to let him learn the hard way. Yet, she came every time, telling him, "Next time, I'm not coming." "If she had stopped somewhere along the line," he said, "I think I would have stopped. But each time, she came."

One of the saddest memories of childhood that he shared with me, however, was that no one had ever stopped him to ask what was wrong with him or what could be done to help him or his family. "I think if someone could have taken the initiative to do that, I could have spared myself, my family and the victims of my crimes a lot of pain." When he finally left home for New York at the age of fifteen, he still carried the dream of earning enough money to move his family of thirteen from the two-room shack in which they lived into a "real house."

Malcolm also carried the grief over his family's hardships that, he felt, had robbed him of his childhood. "People always told me that I was too serious and that playing is something I never did. After leaving that farm, I don't ever remember playing as a child. I don't remember a childhood after that."

⸺⸻⸺

As the Dorm 7 group continued weekly community-building sessions, it became obvious that we had made the right decision in choosing Malcolm to become a group leader. He was forever willing to take risks with the group, to share stories of his own struggles and to give confidence to the other men by proving that it was safe to open up.

The more Rusty and I listened to the stories of the men of Dorm 7, and the more we learned about the culture behind prison walls, the more we realized how different it was when compared to the outside world. I learned that imprisonment changes all the rules of human behavior and, therefore, my interpretations of the events I saw around me were not necessarily accurate. It wasn't that the events occurring in the prison were completely illogical, it was the fact that the rules of logic change in a prison.

At times I felt like an explorer who had wandered into some far-off, exotic land with no cultural understanding of its inhabitants. By this time in my life, however, I knew that the best way to learn about one's *own* culture was to spend time in others'. This first began to be apparent to me when I was stationed in Germany in the U.S. Army. By contrasting that culture to my own, I began to learn on a deeper level about my own country and myself. This awareness intensified for me when I went to the Soviet Union and listened to their ideas and understandings about history and the United States. This is not to say, of course, that their opinions were necessarily correct; but, to the open mind, they offered another perspective from which to form one's own opinions.

An African friend of mine had often told me stories of Western anthropologists who had come to his village over the years and asked for explanations of their customs and rituals. He explained that the West was so out of touch with the meaning of ritual that Western language no longer had words to embody and explain such things. In spite of this, these "scientists" would make and publish assumptions about what they had observed in Africa based upon the logic and thinking of Western culture. In so doing, they invariably concluded that the indigenous cultures were inferior to modern culture. Gradually, I came to understand that, without a deep exploration through story and personal experience, I could very easily make the same errors concerning prison culture. It was *that* different from life on the outside.

This situation reminded me of Honeywell, the beautiful and well-trained golden retriever that belonged to Wellborn Jack, the lawyer whom I had flown to Angola a few years before and the co-owner of my sailplane. During one of the weekly sessions with Dorm 7, I told the following story.

Honeywell was as smart and gentle as any dog I had ever known, a regular nursemaid around children. My friend Wellborn, who was a lawyer, took her everywhere he went, even to his office. She would lie calmly on a cushion in the corner, waiting patiently for walks during the day. On weekends at the airstrip, where we flew our sailplane, he would leash Honeywell to a tiedown while he went soaring into the thermals of warm air above.

On one occasion, as I walked by Honeywell and reached down to pet her, she snapped at me as if I were a complete stranger in the dark of night. Restricting her freedom, even temporarily, I realized, had completely changed her personality. When I carefully unleashed her, she came over to me as always, tail wagging. As I saw the men in the circle all nodding their heads in understanding of what the dog had felt, I understood on a deeper level what prison was doing to them.

As time went on, when I heard about something that happened in the prison, I began, as a matter of self-examination, to first decipher the meaning of the situation according to my own logic. Then, I would seek out Malcolm and sometimes a few of the other men and ask for their interpretations. More often than not, I found myself in gross error.

There was the time, for instance, when a friend of Malcolm's at Angola was granted parole from his third prison sentence for drug dealing. His family was waiting at the front gate of the prison to take him home when they received a message that he had just been arrested for stabbing another prisoner in a fight that he supposedly started.

Some in the outside world might make assumptions such as, "He must have wanted to remain in prison," or, "Anyone that stupid or psychopathic belongs in a prison." Malcolm, however, explained that the man his friend stabbed had stolen an article of clothing from him the night before. In prison, such a transgression requires immediate retaliation or the victim would gain the reputation of someone not to be respected, someone whom others could exploit. Such a soft reputation has led to many men in prison being raped and claimed or even killed.

Having continued his drug use in prison, Malcolm's friend knew that he was still firmly in the grip of his addiction, would not survive on the outside for very long and would probably wind up back in prison with a life sentence as a habitual offender. If he did not "take care of his business" immediately, the person who stole from him would ruin his reputation while he was away, placing his life in peril upon his return. So, according to the logic of prison life, Malcolm's friend saw no other way.

Soon, the implications of my consistent "misunderstandings" became clear. I realized that if I were in charge of a prison and strictly applied my own logic, which was based upon living in a free society where the rules were different, I might often make decisions that would worsen matters instead of resolve them. David B. Truman, of Columbia University, said, "In the complexities of contemporary existence the specialist who is technically skilled but culturally incompetent is a menace."

I also recognized that legislators make this same mistake time and time again when trying to deal with the people and the issues in our prisons. It is commonly said that the lawmakers of this country are too far removed from those who live in poverty to be effective in resolving their problems and that there is not enough open dialogue between these two groups. Our politicians are even more disconnected from those who live in our prisons, and, in this circumstance, there is *no* dialogue. In fact, to the average citizen, an idea such as hearing what life is like in prison or what poverty is like before making policy seems ridiculous. If not for my unique experiences during this research project, I would have felt the same.

A good example of the reality gap between prisoners and the legislatures who literally hold the prisoners' fates in their hands can be seen in the following experience. In 1994, I attended a conference at Angola held by the Lifers Association. Angola is the main penitentiary in Louisiana's penal system and the largest maximum security prison in the United States. At the time of the conference, the state legislature was considering two prison bills put before it. One was to put an end to the "good time" release policy that the department of corrections operated under, and the second was to remove all of the television sets from the prisons statewide.

The Louisiana Department of Corrections was itself against abolishing good time because it was one of the primary mechanisms they had for keeping prisoners under control and on their jobs in Prison Enterprises. The way that good time works is simple: If a prisoner is "good" and works hard, he can shorten his sentence. Corrections officials tried to explain to the politicians that without good time, prisoners would have little incentive to do anything the officials demanded of them. In this matter, all participants at the conference I was attending, including the lifers, agreed with the department of corrections.

When Malcolm got up to speak, he too spoke in support of the good time policy. Then, he made the statement that he wished the department of corrections would take all the television sets in the prison system and "throw them over the fence and burn them." Everyone in the room stood up with applause and cheers. I had suffered a split second of concern at what my neighbors' reactions would be since the audience was not segregated in any way, and I was sitting surrounded by men serving life sentences. As I stood up and joined in the applause for Malcolm, I turned to the man beside me and asked, "Why are we applauding?" The man said, "He's right. They should take all the TVs outta here so these youngsters would spend their free time learnin' to read instead of watchin' that goddamn thing."

By the end of that legislative session, the state had abolished good time but left the televisions.

As at other correctional institutions, violence was all too common at DCI. When I would hear of a brutal beating, a death or a rape somewhere in the prison, Malcolm would help me understand the context in which events happened. "Prison is where I witnessed my first murder," he once told me. "And to this day, I have never witnessed that outside of prison. I had never seen anyone get stabbed or hung until I went to prison, and it was in prison that I witnessed and smelled the burning human flesh of another person because someone set him on fire.

"In Camp J, the maximum punishment camp at Angola, people save their body wastes for months, and they use it as a weapon to throw on someone because they had a disagreement. You have to pass by each other's cells to go shower or go outside. And I'm told that the longer you save it, the more the acid builds up in it. Having somebody throw body waste on me was one of my biggest fears. I mean, it just gives me the shivers to think that someone would do that to me.

"Having a prison guard hit me was another fear of mine, because if they were to do it and I wasn't handcuffed, I know I would strike back, and I know the consequence of that. To simply raise my hand could cost me my life, or could have my body broken up to the point I would never recover.

"At one point, I worked the night shift at the infirmary at Angola, and I would go back to the dorm when it was still dark. There was a time when I walked in after a stabbing and there was blood everywhere. The paramedics were workin' on the guy trying to save his life, and correctional officers were tearing up the place, looking for knives. They knew we all had them.

"Before the federal government made them put correctional officers in the dormitory at night in Angola, we used to sleep with one hand over our throat and a knife taped in the other. We used to actually take books and whatever we could find and make a chest plate out of them because so many guys lost their life while they were sleeping. And you couldn't tuck in the cover on your bed because when someone go to jougging [stabbing] you, then you'd be trapped in the bed and couldn't get up quickly.

"So there was a lot of fear with being in there, and just by the grace of God I have made it this far. I am damaged, though, and will always be scarred by this experience, but I don't think I am as scarred as many people I know."

As I continued to hear these and many other stories in private conversations with Malcolm, they continued to alter my perceptions of prison life and the horrors that incarcerated men had to deal with.

One day I asked Malcolm to tell me more about prison rape. Before I came to DCI, I had heard that rape went on in prison and a few stories about it during the workshop, but I had no idea how widespread the offense was. Even popular movies such as *The Shawshank Redemption*, which seemed to deal honestly with rape, still portrayed it as something that was only practiced by a gang of "aberrant" prisoners. With his usual directness, Malcolm told me how bad things really were.

"One of the most horrible experiences of prison for me," Malcolm said, "was witnessing another man get raped, crying out. And that is a horrible, horrible sound to hear. Not that it's not as horrible for a woman. I have always been sensitive to women being sexually abused or raped, but I have witnessed it happen to a man. And that sound is like hearing a man scream who has been set on fire. I have heard that, too. And the smell of human flesh burning is engraved on my soul. I don't believe I would ever want to get rid of it, because those memories remind me just how cruel we can be to each other as human beings.

"People who get turned out, made into homosexuals, gal boys, can go home and come back ten years later, and they still belong to the person who initially turned them out. And everyone in prison respects that. That guy is still his whore, and he has the right to sell him to someone else to take care of his financial needs or keep him for himself.

"There's definitely a system of prostitution going on in the prison system. There are guys, 'homosexuals,' whose lover [rapist] will make them put him on their family's visitor list and they'll visit together. And these guys will force their homosexuals to tell their family, 'Well, this my ol' man.' They are that cruel. You have families who pay rapists in prison to protect their son. Or they plead with him, 'If he is going to be your homosexual, at least treat him right, don't kill him.' One guy, who had four or five homosexuals at a time, used to make each guy take out his penis and lay it on the table. Then he'd take a shoe and hit it, wham! and say, 'You are no longer a man, you don't need that and you better not never bulldag [have sex] with one of your sisters, or no other homosexual.'

"A lot of homosexuals end up having family members come

into the prison system—brothers, even some fathers. They are ashamed of what they have been forced to become, but they can't get out of that life. Some of them are fortunate enough that their ol' man, their husband, will sell them to their brother or their father or uncle, just to get them out of that life.

"In a prison, if a whore happens to go to the block [maximum security] and get put in a two-man cell together with a stranger who is not a homosexual, that stranger don't have to ask him or force him to have sex with him. The man who has been turned out will probably automatically offer to have sex with him because that's become his role. He feels that way because this stranger knows he is a homosexual, and he knows that he would probably threaten him or force him to do it anyway. So that is another form of rape that occurs in prisons all over this country.

"I don't know of anyone ever being charged with rape in the prison system. In many places, the system encourages it, and there have been times when guys have physically run, I mean, literally ran to the correctional officer for help and been told, 'Get on back down there. Just go on and do what he wants you to do, it ain't goin' to hurt much. Go do what he wants you to do.'

"Not all homosexual activity is forced upon those participatin' in it. Some of the saddest prisoners I know of have been in prison for twenty, thirty years or so without ever havin' a visitor, or receivin' a letter, birthday or Christmas card or gift.

Some of them turn to a homosexual relationship just to get some kind of human love.

"You know, and not for no negative reason, but there was a couple of occasions where I may have asked the nurse in the infirmary to take my blood pressure or my pulse or something just to have the reminder of the touch of a person. And, you know how important that is. Sometimes I know guys would act out just to have somebody touch them."

These stories broke my heart, but the depth of Malcolm's insights into the needs and fears that drove men in prison, and the ways in which he had learned to cope with these horrors, impressed me deeply. An unexpected bond, seemingly different from simple camaraderie, was gradually forming between the two of us. One of us white, one of us black. One free, one not.

By the end of the second month of the research, the men of Dorm 7 requested a significant change of policy. During this time, they had continued to voice their dissatisfaction that their attendance was still mandatory. "Why we *have* to do this?" several of the men grumbled at each session.

Many of the things that the prisoners were expected to do, especially the things that they hated, were mandatory. I guessed that some of the men just wanted the freedom to determine their participation in the workshops. Whatever the reasons, this issue had become so important that Rusty and I decided that, from then on, the men could choose whether or not they wanted to continue the program. This represented a considerable risk. If a significant number of the men decided to drop out, the research process would suffer a major setback. Yet, in light of the growing trust and respect that Rusty and I felt for the men, we no longer felt willing to force the issue.

The following afternoon I announced to the men, "Okay, you want to choose whether or not to participate? We're going to give you the chance. Tonight, Rusty and I will come by your dormitory before supper. On your way to the food line, those of you who want to continue with the program can step into the back room, one at a time, and give us your decision." To our surprise, fifty out of fifty-two decided to remain with the program. Later, the two who dropped out changed their minds and returned.

There were several surprises, not the least of which was Perry Bernard. Perry had been one of the men who had done the most complaining about the overall program, and I was floored that he chose to continue his participation. Standing about five feet, seven inches tall and fairly stocky, Perry was one of the younger members of the group. His job at the prison was to wash cars. The only story he had ever shared in the group was not about his distant past or his childhood, but about an incident that had occurred the previous Saturday morning.

"One of the guards woke me up about six in the morning an' tol' me to go wash some cars. Well, while I was gettin' dressed, I was bitchin' to the guys near my bunk, 'cause I'm not s'posed to wash cars on Saturday. They're only s'posed to work us five days a week. Besides, Saturday is visitor day an' my wife, Juanita, was bringin' our son Bébé to see me. Havin' to work meant that I might not have time to shower before I was called to the visitin' shed." Cleanliness and neatness were very important matters to Perry.

Word of his complaining evidently reached the captain. The next thing Perry knew, he was ordered to report to the Unit 2 administrative area known as the "Front Keys." When he got there, several other officers stood around him as the captain started to hit him hard in his chest, knocking him against the wall. He slapped him several times in his face and taunted him.

"I knew what he wanted," Perry said, "and that was for me to hit him back. That would give all of 'em the excuse to beat the shit out of me. I wanted so bad to hit that man, I wanted to *kill* him, talkin' that shit to me, hittin' me, slappin' me like that. But they'd 'a throwed my ass in the dungeon an' written me up, an' that shit'd show up on my record when I come up for parole, an' I couldn't have that."

Sensing the intensity of Perry's rage, I also recognized a

quickness about his wit and an obvious intelligence. Perry had been very confrontational with Rusty and me during the workshop, but his comments had always been well thought-out and reasonable. What, I wondered, had brought him to abandon that wit and intelligence and end up in prison? When Perry entered the back room and declared his continued commitment to the program, I speculated that by working through some of his rage in the community-building sessions, Perry had, to some extent, regained his connection with his innate capacity for quickness and his ability to reason.

As the weekly community-building workshops progressed, I continued to witness a slow and steady upward curve of trust and mutual esteem in the men of Dorm 7. Life slowly improved in the dormitory as the men began to use the communication skills they developed in the workshop to work out their differences. Men who had lived together in the dorm for years, barely exchanging words, now began to share with each other, sometimes even confessing things that formerly would have put them in positions of dangerous vulnerability. When one prisoner admitted that he was a former narcotics agent, the group accepted him and did not seek retribution as they would have only a few weeks earlier. When another man confessed that he was a closet homosexual, no one in the group tried to rape him or put a claim on him. Even the correctional officers noticed the change in climate, reporting that the men seemed to be carrying on meaningful conversations instead of the usual jive.

As they explored the new experience of being a community, the men discovered useful and productive things about each other. For example, several men found out that their parents and families lived in the same neighborhood. Since some of their family members had cars and others' did not, the men were able to arrange for carpooling on visitors' day. Visitations increased dramatically, which was very positive. Research has long shown that increased visitations decrease violence and the number of infractions of prison rules. In addition, and not surprisingly, seeing loved ones and friends on a more regular basis has a calming effect upon men who are incarcerated.

This carpooling—or more accurately, this type of communication—would have been impossible before the workshop. One of the greatest terrors a prisoner lives with is the fear that an enemy will try to retaliate for a real or imagined wrong, and that his enemy will have a friend on the outside harm or kill a family member. To actually volunteer the location of one's family took extraordinary trust. Over the following months, even marriages (many states allow marriages in prison, the idea being that it stabilizes the individual, both while incarcerated and upon release) increased among the men who were not lifers. Some men told stories of phoning family members who they had not spoken with in years and apologizing for old wrongs.

It wasn't a surprise that these changes brought about a considerable decrease in violence and other major rule infractions within the dormitory. As major infractions decreased, however, minor infractions temporarily increased. The reason for this was simple. As the men learned to respect themselves and to give respect to others, they also began to expect it in return. This meant that when a correctional officer blew off at one of them, the individual would respond by saying, "I don't talk to you like that and I don't want you to talk to me like that." Andrew told a correctional officer, "I don't want to be called Psycho anymore. My name is Andrew Webster."

Since the correctional officers of Dorm 7 did not yet understand what was happening with this group, they took these kinds of comments as insubordination and wrote them up as minor infractions. Once I had determined which of the correctional officers I could reason with and explained to them what was going on, the situation improved.

The aura of extraordinary respect so permeated Dorm 7 that among correctional personnel it soon became one of the most coveted jobs in the prison. On one occasion, I overheard a correctional officer talking to the warden about the change in attitude of the prisoners. "Nowadays, during the count," he said, "when I'm walking back up the aisle, they don't fart." I had to bite my lip to keep from laughing. "Now, that might seem like a small thing to you," he said looking over at me, "but, really, it's not."

For many of the prisoners, the workshop opened up a whole new world. Several reported feeling as if they had been waiting for this for a long, long time. Malcolm told the group that, for him, "The world now seems to have a glow to it, so much brighter than I had ever thought it could be. I can look at myself and see what a great work of art I am and the greatness out of which I was created."

Malcolm also saw that glow on the faces of the other men in Dorm 7. "I've been watching men leave this workshop and go back to the cell block to call loved ones they hadn't spoken to in years. And I ask myself, 'Is this really happening?'"

Many of the prisoners agreed that nothing else had even come close to the natural high they felt after the workshops, the dizzy sensation of walking two feet above the ground. Malcolm admitted that, for him, the feeling was "greater than the high I felt on heroin, and more intense than the euphoria I had the first time I fasted."

Many of the prisoners were concerned how long the effects of the workshop would continue. Many were convinced that the changes would not last. We knew they were right, unless the community-building workshops continued. But they were wrong about the changes within themselves. The years since have shown that, whatever the results of our efforts, none of the men in Dorm 7 ever really lost the intrinsic worth of that experience with us and each other. Whatever light had been turned on inside would stay on.

4 | The Search for Initiation: Remembering the Song of Africa

*A*t the end of the first seven weeks, all three groups were retested for reading ability. When the scores were averaged out, the men of Dorm 7 had collectively improved an entire grade level. It came as no surprise that the two control groups that had not undergone the community-building process showed no improvement, even though one of them had received all of the same reading classes as Dorm 7. In spite of this success, the team knew that we would have to repeat the experiment at least two more times, since scientific research demands that results be replicable. Hopes were high that the outcome would be consistent, but, for the time being, everyone felt like celebrating.

When the men of Dorm 7 heard the good news about their test scores, they asked me to arrange a banquet, something the prison occasionally allowed. I immediately agreed, knowing that rewards are a part of any good behavioral program. A banquet would also give us the opportunity to hand out certificates of achievement that would be useful to the prisoners the next time they appeared before the parole or pardon board.

The banquet was scheduled for a Saturday night, several weeks after the final testing. Many family members would visit that weekend, and, since they could attend as guests, the turnout would be heavy. As the day approached, however, a prison administrator decided to allow the Jimmie Swaggart Ministries to use the facility that night for a revival. We had no choice but to reschedule. Then, on the Saturday before the revival, the warden at DCI and a warden from a nearby prison decided to have their boxing teams fight it out on that same date as the revival. The revival was pushed back a week, and the banquet yet *another* week. How paradoxical that the warden, who boasted of being a devout Christian, should give a violent boxing match precedence over prayer and community.

At DCI, a banquet is a very special event. The food is invariably better than the daily fare. The prisoners can sit side-by-side at a table with their families, and the prison band usually plays. Many of the things I took for granted are considered special treats at a banquet. For example, when I asked the prisoners what they wanted on the menu, the number-one request was green salad. Some men told me that they had not tasted lettuce for over a decade. On the day of the banquet, however, I heard that the lettuce we had ordered was not coming. I jumped into my car and hurried to the only super-market in a nearby town. To my amazement, lettuce was on special. I gave the manager an apologetic look and bought the store's last thirty-nine heads.

During the banquet, Humpty, one of the men who had requested lettuce, came over and thanked me. "I heard about what you done for us when the lettuce didn't come in, and I appreciate that a lot, man. I ain't tasted no lettuce fo' thirteen years. I ain't ate off a plate, instead of a plastic tray, or seen no flowers, or tablecloth, or fresh fruit neither, since I been down." Over and over, Malcolm kept remarking how beautiful the food looked on the plate and how heavy the plate felt in his hands.

In the community-building session that followed the banquet, there was much talk about the long-ago memories that the banquet brought back to the men. Malcolm talked about the time he was transferred from Angola to Hunt Correctional Center. "We passed through LSU and just as we come off the campus, we passed by this store, I think it was a 7-11. The window where I was sitting was open and even with the door of that store. As someone was comin' out, I smelled the fragrance of the place. It had been so long since I had been in a food store, and I wanted so much to go in and just smell that. It's been four years, an' I can still smell dat store."

The highlight of the banquet was the presentation of the certificates of achievement. Each man came forward individually and received his award. As the ceremony progressed, handshakes from Rusty and I turned into hugs. The special award for perfect attendance went to Perry Bernard, the man whom I thought would be the first to drop out of the program when we made participation voluntary. Perry's seven-year-old son Bébé accompanied him to the front of the banquet room to accept this honor, and then Perry led the group in singing the tune they had adopted as their class song, "Lean On Me." Humpty, Clarence and I accompanied the prison band. Some of the men went crazy when they saw me rock with the beat and sing in harmony with the others:

"We all need,

"Somebody,

"To lee-eean on."

Some of the visitors came up to thank us for helping their son, brother or father, and they expressed their hopes that this program would give them the skills they needed to survive on the outside.

Suddenly, the piercing, almost deafening sound of a police whistle subdued the ceremony into instant silence. In the middle of the room stood Captain Murphy, a massive man with a bulge of chewing tobacco on one side of his face and eyes that drooped beneath the dark-blue baseball cap that matched his uniform. He began to angrily shout out orders, "Visitors stand over on one side of the room. Prisoners line up behind me."

The captain's face reflected complete exhaustion and depression. I knew from a prior conversation that he worked three jobs—days on his farm, nights at the prison and week-ends running a convenience store. Perhaps because he worked so hard, he didn't believe that the prisoners deserved a party. Or perhaps he didn't understand the importance for prisoners to maintain close family ties, to show their loved ones how they were progressing and to receive encouragement from them, and how all of that factored into the prisoners' success or failure when reintegrating into free society. Whatever the reason, the celebration was over and everyone was starkly reminded that they were in a prison.

⊸⊶

A year earlier when I had asked Scott Peck if he thought his community-building model could work in prisons, he had answered, "I don't know, Bob. But we'll never find out unless someone tries, and I wish *you'd* try." Now, after much effort by all the participants, prisoners and facilitators, I was encouraged to see the potential of community building unfold in the lives of the men of Dorm 7. Murderers, rapists, bank robbers and drug dealers had made difficult changes. They had moved from a place of profound mistrust of one another—and especially of the two white men who had come into the prison to "fuck around with their heads"—to a place of growing trust and cooperation. The code of extreme isolation that each of them practiced had waned for most.

Our question, "Were prisoners capable of building community together?" had been amply answered, but none of us had any illusions about this work being a seven-week wonder. The program participants had not turned into spiritually enlightened New-Agers, but they had undergone a profound shift. They still had an abundance of problems, but they were learning more effective ways to solve them. I found myself wishing that I could better understand the reasons behind these transformations. If I could, I felt that I would be able to offer the prisoners much more of what they needed.

I understood that the primary element of this new experience of community building was a certain sensibility that Scott Peck called "extraordinary respect," a term first used by Peck in his book *The Different Drum*. For the vast majority of participants, to be treated with respect and dignity as a human being—in spite of the terrible crimes that many of them had committed—was a completely new experience, and for many, it was a life-transforming event. No one—not their parents, teachers, principals, the police and certainly not prison officials—had ever treated them like this on a consistent basis. When the men of Dorm 7 consistently received this respect, they gained respect for themselves and others. The bottom line is: If you want to get respect from men in prison, first you have to give it. That doesn't guarantee that you will get it, but it by far represents your best chance. This is probably true anywhere, and nowhere is it more true than in prison.

Another important part of the puzzle was the dramatic release of emotional blocks. While I understood that the men ultimately had to learn how to solve their own problems, I also knew that someone who is in the grip of a paralyzing emotion or crisis is often unable to think clearly enough to come up with a workable solution. It does not matter what the emotion is. Fear, rage, love, grief—or even joy—can block one's ability to function rationally. My father once told me, "Never make an important decision if you are very angry or very happy."

My flight instructor, Hugh Hunton, told me repeatedly during my pilot training, "If something goes wrong with your aircraft, count to ten before you do anything." Counting to ten requires the brain to block out emotion and compels its return to the mode of thinking instead of feeling. Many pilots have lost their aircraft because they panicked and just did not think.

I had to use this lesson once when I lost all power in my single-engine airplane. My first impulse was to call the tower and shout, "May Day!" to the controller, but, somehow, I remembered my instructor's words. By the time I had counted to five, several things had become very clear: One, I was not going to get my engine back; two, I had already passed the grass landing strip north of the airport; and, three, there was an interstate highway—the "world's longest runway"—just ahead that I could land on if I couldn't make the airport. If forced to land there, I could at least do so without hurting my airplane or myself. I also realized that I could take advantage of the fifteen-knot tailwind the tower had just reported, the two thousand feet of altitude I had and my expertise at flying "engineless" airplanes. I originally learned to fly in sailplanes and had made over one hundred landings with no engine.

By forcing myself to keep my wits about me, I was able to land my plane safely at the airport within the normal traffic pattern and keep enough speed to coast all the way to my hanger. I never declared an emergency.

However, counting to ten does not always enable one to put aside the perpetual crises of everyday life in prison; nor could it help overcome the lifetime of unreleased emotions that most of the people in our prisons—and many who live in free society—are so filled with that they are unable either to think clearly or to move forward.

The shame of failure—of being labeled a criminal; of not being able to live the way a man is supposed to live and provide for his family; of not being a part of society; of being thrown away—is a heavy burden to bear. Add to these failures the physical and psychological warfare that goes on in prisons—the threat of being raped, sold, traded, beaten and extorted. All of these things create an individual who, once released, is hard put to think rationally and resolve conflict in nonviolent ways; find a job; take responsibility for himself; or survive the complexities of modern society.

The prisoners in Dorm 7 continued undergoing dramatic transformations. The ongoing workshops provided them, for the first time, with a safe environment in which to discharge more and more intense emotions. One prisoner, Charles, described his profound relief after one community-building session. "This is a thousand times better than confession."

To bring myself closer to the men and gain a greater cultural understanding, I joined with them in disclosing my own brokenness and failures, even confessing my former racist attitudes and behaviors that were, despite my parents' views of equality, an inevitable consequence of growing up in the segregated South. Though sharing them was potentially alienating or even explosive, I felt I could not lead the men toward a deeper community if I was not willing to go down with them. As a result, they opened up to me and I bore witness to worse things than I had ever imagined could happen to a person and to the worst things that they had ever done.

Malcolm, meanwhile, continued to keep me aware of the invisible elements of prison life that an outsider could not see. I once asked him why *he* thought the workshops were having such dramatic results. He explained to me that most of the men were ripe for such changes and they simply needed a safe and respectful environment. For many men and women, Malcolm explained, prison provides the first chance they have ever had to sit down and try to figure out who they are and what went wrong. In between moments of self-examination, however, they spend much of their time just trying to survive. A large majority, if not all, of the people coming out of prison are motivated not to go back. Without proper support, however, transformation is a long hard road. Because most of them are unprepared, most of them fail. Our prisons provide and perpetuate the antithesis of an environment where the prisoners can use their new insights to mend their broken lives and move forward.

Malcolm further attributed the success of the program to the fact that Rusty and I came to DCI and broke all the rules, especially the ones that said, "Men don't talk about their real troubles in prison. They don't come together and try to help each other. They don't cry, and they especially don't hug each other."

With great satisfaction, I recorded the behavioral transformations of the men in Dorm 7 as I experienced my own dramatic evolution in the way I looked at the world. I began to see from a completely different perspective what it meant to be incarcerated. I began to more clearly perceive the absurdity of society's view that prisoners were largely unredeemable criminals who could not be turned back into productive, law-abiding citizens. I could see the potential to reclaim these men as valuable human resources, if only I could implement a program that could effectively tap this potential. I resolved to create such a program.

———

Another significant change was brewing in my life. I had begun to share my journey with a new person, Rosemary Mumm. I had met her two years before on my trip to the Soviet Union. Rosie had come to Moscow from Woodstock, Illinois, near Chicago, with the civilian diplomacy organization that sponsored the gathering. As a specialist in the treatment of drug dependency, she led one of the small groups on the theme of addictions as we cruised down the Volga River. I was quickly attracted to her lovely smile, tongue-in-cheek humor and full-bodied laughter. On the last night of our Soviet odyssey, we attended the Leningrad Symphony. Afterward, we talked until early the following morning about what lay in store for us if we pursued our budding relationship further. I thought it impossible and left Russia the next day with no intention of seeing her again. But, before I reached home, I knew it was not over and tried to call her from New York. When I finally reached her, she had just walked in the door. Luckily, she felt the same as I did—we had unfinished business together.

During our correspondence and conversations over the

next months, we found enchantingly common themes in our spiritual journeys, and we fell in love. Rosie also became a valuable resource for me as I strove to learn about the subtleties of addictive behavior.

As partners, we decided to begin our early years working together on my research. My experiences were so intense that there would have been no way to fully relate to her all my transformations by simply talking about them. If we did not experience them together, I felt I could not really tell her who I was becoming. The experiences we shared changed us, forever deepening our relationship in wonderful ways.

When Rusty and I first discussed Rosie joining our team, we felt it best not to include her in the community-building workshops. We limited her role to data management and working with the men on addiction issues and in the reading program. We feared the community-building sessions would be no place for a woman.

After the first two community-building experiences, however, Rusty and I no longer had any such concerns. The only problem was that the men developed a respect for her that soon evolved into adoration, which meant they wouldn't *get real* in her presence. At one point during an early workshop, she coughed and four men got up to get her a glass of water. It was not that the men had not seen or spoken to a woman since being locked up. Everyday they saw women who worked at the prison. But to have a woman trust and care about them and to be real and honest about her own life, as Rosie did and was, was for some their first such experience.

The problem with Rosie's presence became most apparent on the first day of a new community-building group from Dorm 1. The men were reluctant to swear in her presence. We knew that this meant they were holding themselves back and not expressing their full range of emotions. True rage cannot be expressed without four-letter words.

When one young man finally broke through the layer of politeness in the course of his grief work, he began to talk sorrowfully about how he had to "suck ass." "All my life, I just been suckin' ass," he said.

An older member of the group nudged him to get his attention. "Say, man, there's a lady present," he told him uneasily. The group froze into a fretful and uncertain silence.

Finally, Rosie responded. Following the guidelines of community building, she said her name before speaking, "Well, my name is Rosie, and, Ronald, I hope you don't have to suck ass much more in your life." The room roared with laughter as Rosie broke the ice so that the men could get on with their struggle to face the events that had devastated their lives.

A year later Rosie and I married with blessings, well wishes and predictions of happiness from all the men. Before we departed for our wedding ceremony in Woodstock, the men of Dorm 1 presented us with a wooden plaque that one of them had crafted and finished. On it were the men's names and grateful words for the work we had done with them. Upon our return, the men greeted us like family and insisted on seeing the photographs of our wedding and honeymoon in Oregon before we settled back down to the business of their reading classes. A few days later, I was struck deeply when they mentioned that these kinds of events reminded them of their loss of such freedoms. Yet they could still express such joy over the stories of our travels.

A few weeks after our return to work, I was walking back to the compound from a reading session with Clarence Williams, one of the Dorm 7 participants. I stopped dead in my tracks as he told me that, as a youth, he had believed that "prison was the place where I would go to become a man."

I felt completely taken aback. Since my first days at the prison, I noticed that prisoners often acted like children who *needed* to become men. During initial meetings with prison correctional officers and administration personnel, I was told to expect this. *Of course they act like children*, I thought, given my earlier experience at Angola. *That's what everyone demands and expects.*

Now, Clarence had added a new, complicated dimension to my thinking and the question, "How does a boy become a man? Could the process of becoming a man happen in a prison?" The term "initiation" began to swirl in my head. One dark truth behind my question was that even I was profoundly unsure of what being a man really meant. So how the hell was I ever going to teach manhood to anyone else?

Fortuitously, someone sent Rusty an audiotape of the famous poet/activist/author Robert Bly's *The Naive Male*, in which Bly spoke about becoming a man.[3] We listened to the tape on our way to the prison one morning. Bly went straight to the heart of the question every male asks himself at some time in his life, "What does it mean to be a man?" I had seen Hollywood's answer and knew I was neither John Wayne nor Charlton Heston. Bly spoke of how the patriarchy has left the contemporary male emotionally numb and naive, especially about women, and that our macho veneer is a pitiful attempt to cover all that. Bly then pointed to the indigenous world and ancient myths to illustrate traditions of true manhood that are as old as human existence. I decided that this was the direction in which I would begin my quest for more answers.

In the mail soon after, I received a brochure about the next Minnesota Men's Conference. When I saw that Bly would be leading the conference, along with drummer/storyteller/mythologist Michael Meade and the extraordinary psychologist/author James Hillman, I made plans to attend. I did not know what to expect from this "Gathering of Men," but I knew that I wanted (and perhaps needed) to be there.

The gathering was unlike anything I had ever experienced. In all my years of attending retreats, seminars and community-building workshops, I had never attended a conference just for men. One hundred-fifty men met in the woods of Brainerd, Minnesota, to deal with the ashes of the patriarchy,

how it has left us living in a desert that we call modern culture, and the damage it has inflicted upon our natural souls.
We talked about our culture's inability to grieve and about the
mysterious connection between that incapacity and the
numbness that many men feel today. I remember thinking
that the only way I had avoided such numbness was through
the overstimulating effects of racing and stunt flying.

There in Minnesota, men had gathered for the previous six
years to recreate a process that had long been lost in the
Western cultures of Europe. Well-versed in the indigenous ways
of Native Americans and Africans, the conference leaders and
participants had become quite accomplished at community
building through grief work. Following the introductions of the
conference leaders and their opening remarks, Bly asked the
assembly of men to stand up individually, say their name and
answer a simple question: "What failure brought you here?"

Within half an hour, we were sharing on a level as deep
as any I had ever known—a level that other groups in
which I had participated had taken many hours, and, in the
case of one of my therapy training groups, several months
to accomplish.

The entire six days and nights were filled with brilliant lectures, poetry, debate, singing, dancing, drumming, laughing
and grieving. Once again, I felt the satisfaction of having a
deep longing inside me met. Sometimes my grief was about
how much of my life I had lived without such gatherings of

men. Bly's poetry, lectures and humor were electrifying. He was at times the benevolent grandfather, and at others the stern instructor.

Meade told an ongoing story each night while playing his drum. This Russian fairy tale, *The Firebird*, had been handed down through generations over thousands of years. It involved the perilous journey of a young hunter who rides a horse of power, marries a beautiful woman and becomes a king. Each character in the story represented an energy or trait that each of us carries within—the king, the warrior, the magician, the lover. The story implied that true manhood requires us to cultivate all these characteristics in ourselves. Dr. Robert Moore published a brilliant book that explains these energies in detail, *King, Warrior, Magician, Lover*.

Hillman spoke brilliantly of the soul as our true genius, whose commands we feel as desires and longings to fulfill an intention or purpose in our lives. I wondered if perhaps my soul had created the desire that turned me from dentistry towards this path I now pursued.

In the course of the gathering, Bly talked about the value of conflict in creating true community. With this in mind, he set aside time during the course of each day for intentional conflict. "Throughout history," he explained, "men have never really been able to trust one another until faced with an opportunity for violence that was passed over."[4]

This gave me a much different perspective about the potentially explosive confrontations that had almost materialized in the DCI workshops. This had been the prisoners' way of testing the waters with one another—a way of building an environment of trust that there would be no violence in the circle. Moreover, while intentional conflict was perhaps an important factor for a gathering of men in Minnesota, working through conflict was quintessential for building an environment of true community among men in prison.

During the conference, I also jotted down a section of a poem on conflict by Emily Dickinson.

> the palate of the hate departs; . . .
> Anger as soon as fed is dead;
> 'Tis starving makes it fat.

Bly, Hillman and Meade all spoke about the need for initiation. "Men," Meade said, "are eruptive by nature and have a natural brutality and quality of dangerousness."

Everything depends upon how this "dangerousness" is put to use. Though the particulars vary from tradition to tradition, an essential component of initiation is teaching a young man how to harness this vital energy so that he can learn how to express it in a positive sense, by becoming "dangerous" in ways that serve himself, his family, his community and Earth. For example, in our culture, an initiated man might be someone who will fight not only for his own rights, but for women's rights. He might refuse to work for a company that supports policies that despoil the environment. An initiated man is a person of principle who will speak out against (become dangerous to) whatever threatens his community—which might well be such enemies as pollution, racism, sexism or oppression.

Throughout the conference, I wished with all my heart that I could offer the men from DCI something like this "Gathering of Men." In a real sense, I realized Clarence could be right—prison *could* be a place where a boy could become a man. Our prisons hold tremendous potential to be places of initiation. All of the ancient patterns are there: boys (uninitiated men) are taken from their homes and the village to a place where there are only men present. In this place they undergo certain physical, emotional and spiritual tests that they either pass or fail.

If the men in prison could pass their own versions of these tests, if they could find their mentors and elders among the older men who had learned how to do their time with dignity and strength, if they could find self-worth in their study of black and African history, if they could refuse to surrender their dignity to the brutalization of the system, they could break through—as Malcolm had, as the men in Dorm 7 were doing—to their very souls. They could truly find their way to a life of integrity, courage and dignity.

Deeply stirred by this realization, I grieved that this great potential was wasted since our prisons were not places of initiation but places of humiliation, senseless cruelty, violence and rape. Now that I had caught this vision I somehow had to find a way to bring it more powerfully into our work at DCI.

———

I felt that my next step along this journey was to learn more about initiation, and to learn it from an African. When I first began my work at DCI, I believed that my upbringing had uniquely prepared me to understand and relate to African-Americans—those earliest days on that farm in the deep South; my relationship with Parrie, who had raised me when my mother was at work and who had become a second mother to me; at age sixteen, when I began my first of five summers working side by side with the African-American men at the warehouse, men who had been kind and encouraging while I struggled through the grueling seventy-two hour workweeks and the boss's constant flow of insults.

Remembering those experiences, I assumed that I knew plenty about being around African-Americans. But a voice inside of me—the one that kept calling out to me about initiation—also told me that I needed to know about the indigenous soul of Africa. In order to affect the men at DCI at the level I was imagining, I would have to acquire radically different experiences far beyond those of merely growing up around African-Americans.

First, I began to read everything I could by black authors. I wanted to know what was inside the hearts and souls of these African-American men that even five hundred years of slavery had not destroyed. I felt not only ready, but hungry, for more understanding of indigenous Africa, for knowledge that was perhaps thousands of years old. I also was hungry for the things I felt inside, things that I intuitively knew had once flourished in the cultures of Europe thousands of years ago, qualities of life that had been forgotten for so long that when Europeans found them again among the indigenous tribes of North America, they could no longer recognize them and, therefore, could not re-assimilate them. Author D. H. Lawrence said, "What a culture cannot assimilate, it will destroy."

It is said that when the student is ready, the teacher will appear. During a 1990 trip to Washington, D.C., where Rosie and I had been invited to speak on community building in prison at the National Institute of Justice, I was given a flyer announcing the first multicultural Men's Conference. It would be held at Buffalo Gap, West Virginia, in the spring of 1991. Realizing that the Men's Movement was in danger of becoming the White Men's Movement, Robert Bly and Michael Meade had raised $80,000 in scholarship money so that men of color who could not afford the tuition could

attend the conference. They had also made sure that half of
the slated conference leaders were black.

Among these speakers was a West African medicine man.
His biography in the brochure read as follows:

> *Malidoma Somé was raised in a village in Burkina Faso,*
> *West Africa. He is initiated in the ancestral tribal traditions,*
> *and is a medicine man and diviner in the Dagara culture.*
> *Malidoma holds three Master's degrees and two Ph.D. degrees*
> *from the Sorbonne and Brandeis University. He has taught*
> *African and Comparative Literature at the University of*
> *Michigan at Ann Arbor and is the recent author of* Ritual:
> Power, Healing and Community.

When I read this description, I knew that I had found
another important teacher. Robert Bly, Michael Meade, James
Hillman—all my favorites—were going to be present, as well
as the Chicago poet, activist and author Haki Madhubuti,
renowned African drummer Aidoo Mamadi Holmes and distinguished playwright Joseph Walker.

When the week of the conference arrived, I was not disappointed. Men from eleven different countries attended the
gathering. Even more gratifying was the fact that one of my
sons, Jeff, decided to go with me. The diversity of participants
brought a divergence of issues and, therefore, more conflict.
The issue of trust took on greater importance than ever. Haki

Madhubuti addressed the crux of the question as soon as he was introduced. "There are certain people here I have to trust—the cooks, the man who sleeps next to me; but I also have to trust Robert Roberts because he brought his son, and I have to trust John Densmore because he came here with two black men whose passage to the conference he has paid."

Haki's words did not lessen the conflicts that would arise, but they kept the gathering focused on trust, the essential factor that could ultimately help us to complete the task ahead of us—that of becoming a multicultural community of men.

At the first opportunity, I introduced myself to Malidoma. I told him briefly about our work, why I had been looking for a teacher and that he was the main reason I had come. I felt an unexpected instant rapport with him. When I explained to him that Louisiana's prison population was 92 percent black (in spite of a 30 percent black population in the state), he was shocked and said, "You build your prisons for black people!" Nevertheless, he gave me his blessing and told me that he saw a lot of good work ahead for me.

In Malidoma's first lecture of the week, he spoke about the dignity and wisdom of his people. I felt as if I were hearing him from that place deep within, where I had heard these things before. Perhaps this is the part of me that I inherited from my Cherokee ancestors. It was as if I were remembering truths that I had always known.

Malidoma began by saying, "It is through pain that I became what I am today." He went on to tell the story of being stolen from his village at the age of four by the Jesuit priest who had befriended his father. Along with hundreds of other kidnapped West African children, he was held prisoner in the Jesuit seminary at Nanci in Burkina Faso, where the boys were indoctrinated with a European education and trained to be priests. While at Nanci, Malidoma and the other boys were raped by the priests. They were punished when they spoke their own languages, and they were told to forget their culture because Africans were dirty, backward people. Fifteen years later, at the age of nineteen, he escaped and walked 120 miles back to his village.

Once there, he discovered that he no longer remembered his culture or his language. To let him become part of the village again, the elders offered him a chance at initiation. Malidoma spoke at length about what it felt like to undergo this challenging ordeal and the lessons he had learned about his true nature. As he spoke, the men present could hardly contain their enthusiasm. They wept, groaned and cried out their encouragement for him to keep going, they laughed at his comments about the crazy contradictions of Western culture. At the end of his talk, Malidoma received a five-minute standing ovation.

The entire conference was taped, and I was overjoyed that I would be able to bring Malidoma's words back to the men at

DCI. Here was someone who had not only come to share the wisdom of indigenous Africa, but who had also suffered so many of the things that the men at DCI had endured: imprisonment, rape, brutality and denigration of one's cultural values. On top of this, a good portion of Malidoma's talk had been about the meaning of indigenous initiation and the knowledge that could be learned from the elders. I was profoundly stirred by what I had heard and I was eager to share and discuss the conference with Malcolm, the other men of Dorm 7 and the new group undergoing community-building, Dorm A.

My other high point of the multicultural conference was the drumming workshop given by the renowned African-American drummer Aidoo Mamadi Holmes. Aidoo was a patient teacher who insisted on sincerity, effort and respect for the drums and rhythms he taught. His hands were thick and hardened from years of playing, yet they were so quick that, at times, they seemed to disappear. The drum he primarily played was the jimbe, a West African drum carved from a tree trunk into an uneven hourglass shape. Its top is covered with a goat skin that is pulled tight by a woven pattern of grass ropes and knots.

Another drum that Aidoo used in the workshop was the joun joun. Made from a large, red metal oil drum, it had cow skins stretched over the top and bottom. The edges of the skins were folded over metal rings that hugged the top and bottom and were held tightly by a woven pattern of knotted rope. The long, deep sounds of the joun joun provided a foundation for the rhythms of all the other drums, and the joun joun could be heard all over the camp. If the joun joun drummer paused for any reason during a drumming beat, all of the other drummers would swerve their heads around immediately to see what had happened to him.

After my first men's conference, I had begun drumming in earnest and continued to study with Luther Gray in New Orleans at Congo Square. This square was the only place in the country where slaves had been allowed to practice their ritual drumming. I had learned that any emotion could be put into this rhythmic pounding: anger, rage, eruptiveness, brutality, competitiveness, violence, courage, upstandingness, wildness, idealism. After a drumming session, I almost always felt released and cleansed and filled with a sense of soulful, peaceful harmony. It is said that there is no sound in the world like the shared silence at the end of a drumbeat.

Sitting in Aidoo's workshop, I felt a burning desire to bring drumming back with me into the prison. I wanted to share that high—that soulful, peaceful harmony of mind and rhythm—with the men at DCI. As my group finished practicing the three parts of an African/Jamaican beat called *Manjani*, I found myself speaking of that dream with the other drummers.

Later, as I was leaving the session, a man walking alongside me asked, "Were you serious about what you said back there?"

Surprised, I answered, "Yes."

"Well, maybe I can help you to make it a reality. My name is John, and I've been a drummer for most of my life. Drumming has been of great benefit to me, and has made me a good living. Now, what I'd really like is the chance to give something back." He said that he would like to purchase some drums for me and asked how many I needed.

I stopped dead in my tracks, hardly believing what I was hearing, but I could see that John was serious. As I tried to answer him, the moment turned into a blur of emotions for both of us. We agreed to get together later and talk more about the idea.

Back at my cabin, I found my roommate and new friend, Brandon, resting on the bunk next to mine. When Brandon, a six-foot, five-inch, very slender, black lawyer from Washington saw my eyes, he asked if I was okay. I sat down and told him everything I could remember about the conversation. When I told him that the guy's name was John and described him, Brandon said, "Man, you know who he is, huh? That's John Densmore, the drummer for The Doors." Densmore was also the man Haki had said he had to trust, because John had come to the conference with two black men whose expenses he had paid. I was surprised that someone so famous would introduce himself without any of his titles or credentials. When I introduced him to my son, John began their conversation by asking Jeff all about himself.

The gathering at Buffalo Gap ended with a banquet and toasts followed by an evening of poetry, hilarious skits by the different small groups, drumming and dancing. It became a pivotal experience in my new life as I continued to build my new relationships with Robert Bly, Malidoma Somé, John Densmore, Haki Madhabuti and many of the conference participants.

—◦◦◦◦◦◦—

John Densmore was as good as his word. Using Aidoo as an agent, he spent $11,000 to purchase twenty drums, including Latin quintes, cungas and tumbas, and four African jimbes. He also sent along twenty other rhythm instruments including clavés, cabasas, bongos, tambourines, cowbells and shekeries. As determined as Aidoo was that the drumming be done well, John offered to pay Aidoo's expenses if he would come to DCI and do an initial drumming workshop for the men to get them started.

The only remaining obstacle was getting permission to hold this workshop. A reluctant Warden Cain said we would have to consult with the secretary of corrections, Bruce Lynn. Because I was unsure of how to explain to Secretary Lynn why I wanted to bring forty drums and rhythm instruments into the prison, and I was unwilling to lie to him, I chose to describe the workshop as "stress therapy" and "emotional-release therapy." Although the whole idea probably sounded cockamamy, to Secretary Lynn's eternal credit he approved it.

READER/CUSTOMER CARE SURVEY

BB1

We care about your opinions. Please take a moment to fill out this Reader Survey card and mail it back to us.
As a special **"thank you"** we'll send you exciting news about interesting books and a valuable **Gift Certificate.**

Please PRINT using ALL CAPS

First Name		MI.		Last Name	

Address |⎍⎍⎍⎍⎍⎍⎍⎍⎍⎍⎍⎍⎍⎍⎍⎍⎍|

City |⎍⎍⎍⎍⎍⎍⎍⎍⎍| ST |⎍⎍| Zip |⎍⎍⎍⎍⎍| — |⎍⎍⎍⎍|

Phone # (|⎍⎍⎍|) |⎍⎍⎍| — |⎍⎍⎍⎍| Fax # (|⎍⎍⎍|) |⎍⎍⎍| — |⎍⎍⎍⎍|

Email |⎍⎍⎍⎍⎍⎍⎍⎍⎍⎍⎍⎍⎍⎍⎍⎍⎍⎍|

(1) Gender:
_____ Female   _____ Male

(2) Age:
_____ 12 or under   _____ 40-59
_____ 13-19   _____ 60+
_____ 20-39

(3) Marital Status
_____ Married
_____ Single
_____ Divorced/Widowed

(4) Did you receive this book as a gift?
_____ Yes   _____ No

(5) How many Health Communications books have you bought or read?
_____ 1   _____ 2-4   _____ 5+

(6) How did you find out about this book?
Please fill in ONE.
1) _____ Recommendation
2) _____ Store Display
3) _____ Bestseller List
4) _____ Online
5) _____ Advertisement
6) _____ Catalog/Mailing
7) _____ Interview/Review (TV, Radio, Print)

(7) Where do you usually buy books?
Please fill in your top TWO choices.
1) _____ Bookstore
2) _____ Religious Bookstore
3) _____ Online
4) _____ Book Club/Mail Order
5) _____ Price Club (Costco, Sam's Club, etc.)
6) _____ Retail Store (Target, Wal-Mart, etc.)

(9) What subjects do you enjoy reading about most? Rank only *FIVE*. Use 1 for your favorite, 2 for second favorite, etc.

	1	2	3	4	5
1) Parenting/Family	○	○	○	○	○
2) Relationships	○	○	○	○	○
3) Recovery/Addictions	○	○	○	○	○
4) Health/Nutrition	○	○	○	○	○
5) Christianity	○	○	○	○	○
6) Spirituality/Inspiration	○	○	○	○	○
7) Business Self/Help	○	○	○	○	○
8) Teen Issues	○	○	○	○	○
9) Sports	○	○	○	○	○

(14) What attracts you most to a book?
(Please rank 1-4 in order of preference.)

	1	2	3	4
1) Title	○	○	○	○
2) Cover Design	○	○	○	○
3) Author	○	○	○	○
4) Content	○	○	○	○

TAPE IN MIDDLE; DO NOT STAPLE

BUSINESS REPLY MAIL

FIRST-CLASS MAIL   PERMIT NO 45   DEERFIELD BEACH, FL

POSTAGE WILL BE PAID BY ADDRESSEE

HEALTH COMMUNICATIONS, INC.
3201 SW 15TH STREET
DEERFIELD BEACH FL 33442-9875

FOLD HERE

Comments:

Once permission came through, I fully realized that I was climbing way out on a limb. There was nothing in the "scientific" or research literature to support drumming as a treatment modality (and there still is not). The drumming workshops had been nothing more than a dream, but now the dream was about to come true. Would it become a nightmare? Would this idea work? Could the men from Dorm 7 really get something from drumming and stories about Africa? Or would I end up looking like a complete idiot?

The drums arrived, and a week later the day of the drumming workshop was upon us. Remembering the deep bass sound of the joun joun, I had been collecting all the materials for building one. The prison meatpacking plant had given me the hide of a recently slaughtered bull, and the day before the workshop Aidoo and I had scraped off the meat and fat (a task that required a strong stomach). We treated the skin and cut it into two large round spheres for the drum heads. I had also purchased a fifty-five–gallon oil drum, cut off the top and bottom, and welded legs onto it.

On the day of the workshop, Aidoo showed the men how to fold the edges of the skins into the four metal rings that I had made for the top and bottom of the drum. With remarkable patience, Aidoo took two hundred feet of rope and taught each of the men how to tie the knots onto the rings and then weave the rope from top to bottom. A different pair of hands tied each knot that went into making the drum.

The workshop was a great success. The men would drum for awhile, then Aidoo would tell stories about the places he had visited in Africa on many occasions. That evening, like children sitting at the feet of an elder listening to tales of their ancestors, the entire group sat in the chapel while Aidoo drummed and shared more stories. The men asked basic questions such as, "What do people wear in Africa? How do men talk to women? What is a typical day like?"

When I heard these questions, I dismissed all the concerns I had harbored about the wisdom of bringing this workshop into the prison. My confidence rose again that night. As I watched the men respond to Aidoo, it was as if I were seeing people who had been separated from their place of birth for years asking, "Who am I? What is my home like?" This was the stuff of initiation—the kind of experience that *should* be happening in prisons. I was reminded of the time when Malcolm told me that he had never felt any self-esteem until he began to learn about the history and the people of Africa as told by Africans, and not by Western anthropologists.

One story that Aidoo shared had an especially strong impact on the men. "In the tribe I belong to in West Africa," he told them, "a man would never hit his wife. If he did, he would receive a visit from the council of elders. The elders would explain to him that if he ever hit her again, they would take her away from him and send her back to her parents, nor would he ever be allowed to have another wife."

Watching the men, I realized that Aidoo's tales were the teaching stories about life that had been stolen from the slave ancestors of the men in the room. At last, these words were finding their way back into the place where they belonged. I was also sharply reminded of something that Malidoma had said at the Buffalo Gap Conference, that by healing oneself, a person was also healing his ancestors and his children. After the workshop, Malcolm came up to me, his eyes filled with quiet joy, and said, "Do you have any idea how important this is?"

The workshop had been so successful that I asked Secretary Lynn for his blessing and protection to keep it going as a regular African studies program on Tuesday nights. He agreed, but Warden Cain insisted on one condition—a correctional officer had to be present at each meeting. I was not happy with this arrangement, but accepted it. In a sense, I understood the warden's concern. Africa was a warrior continent, and I was reintroducing a room predominantly full of African-American men to their history and to the powerful emotional release of drumming.

At the first gathering, before the drumming got underway, I picked up a drum, turned to the black correctional officer who showed up, and said, "Would you like to join us?" Even though the man declined, I was certain that it was appropriate to make the offer. The whole idea of community was to exclude no one. If the correctional officer chose to exclude himself, that was his decision, and not the group's. When the men began to drum, however, I could tell that the correctional officer was enjoying himself.

For this first of our weekly drumming/African studies session, I had brought with me the tape of Malidoma's lecture at Buffalo Gap. The prisoners listened very closely and, I noticed, so did the correctional officer. Malidoma's words had special meaning for the prisoners because, like them, he too had suffered the brutality of imprisonment—and he had survived. He took obvious pride in being African and in the ways of his people, the Dagara, a tribe half a million strong. Sharing the strength a boy gets from risking his life in initiation, Malidoma gave the men a revolutionary new definition of manhood, one that was far removed from the violence and competitiveness of the streets. "If you have power," Malidoma said, "you don't have to show off. If you don't have power, you do."

The men laughed out loud when Malidoma talked about going to Western schools for twelve years. "My elders asked me to go back to school because they needed somebody to go out and talk to the Europeans about our culture. After two Ph.D.s, two master's degrees, and four bachelor's degrees, I decided that there was nothing there for me to learn. The only things worth knowing had been learned at the feet of my elders." He shared the Dagara's vision that each person's life matters. In his tribe, each baby who comes into the world is greeted as a precious, omniscient soul. The Dagara's belief that each life is essential to the survival of the community is vigorously practiced. When the people in the village notice that one of their members has become alienated or is spending too much time alone, they draw that person back into the village by doing a water ritual. The person who has become isolated is asked to sit in a circle and the people all gather around and "call" to that person, saying, "We need you to come back among us. Without your unique gifts we are weaker than we were. When you return to us, we will be strong and whole again, because you have brought a gift to us from the ancestors that only you can give."

Since we come into the world already "knowing" everything we need to know, our purpose in life is to "remember" our life's mission. "We need to understand who we are and what energies we carry around inside of us. Self-knowledge helps us to understand others."

These were healing words to men trying to transform their lives and find dignity in the brutal and humiliating environment of prison. To those who had spent all their lives in a culture that judges people according to skin color, education and economic status, it was a revelation to hear a native African telling them that their ancestors were people who saw each individual life as essential to the survival of the community and believed that respect for self and others was paramount. As the men listened to Malidoma's words, I felt as if they were discovering what my friend, Mayan shaman Martín Prechtel, calls "the unique song within each being that everything in creation sings." The drumming and stories of Africa seemed to free up that unique song in the heart of each man present, the melody that only he could sing, the unique gifts that were his alone to offer. Each was taken closer to his ancestors, his soul, his cultural history and personal past.

The drumming added to this cultural pride. Many of the rhythms from Congo Square that I taught the men had historical connections to slavery and the refusal of black men to be crushed by their enslavement. One of these rhythms, known as *Ibo* (pronounced "ee-boh"), originated with the African slaves who had been brought to New Orleans from the Ibo tribe. Rather than submit to slavery, many of these men would throw themselves over the edge of the boat, shouting "Ibo!" The *Ibo* beat still survived in New Orleans' Congo Square, and I had learned it there. There was a terrific surge of energy in the sound of fifty prisoners drumming and clapping together in a room and then all stopping together at the pause to shout, "Ibo," the cry of slaves plunging to their freedom in the spirit world.

When the session was over, the prisoners, escorted by correctional officers, headed up "the walk." Though I followed at some distance, their rhythmic euphoria was palpable. As the men were led toward the sally port, I heard one correctional officer scream, "Shut up!" Everyone immediately fell silent. Once they were inside the sally port, the correctional officers began to strip-search everyone. Their shouts continued to remind the men (and me) that they were still in a prison where such feelings should not exist. I learned the next morning that they had been held in the bullpen for several hours following the strip searches, and they had not gotten back to the their dorms until around two the next morning.

This incident was not an isolated one. The correctional officers began to consistently put obstacles in the prisoners' way to keep them from getting to the community-building, literacy and drumming workshops. They kept them standing in the sun, the rain or the cold for hours. Each time I heard about this, I would talk to the warden in hopes of gaining his genuine support. I knew this would not happen, however, if I went over the warden's head, to Secretary Lynn, about the problem. All I could do was hope that the warden would eventually honor my effort to show him respect. Following these talks, the correctional officers would lay off for awhile, but soon return to their previous patterns of harassment.

One of the regulars at the African studies program was Randy, known to his friends as Country. Though he lived in Dorm 7 and could not read, he could not participate in the community and literacy program because he worked at Warden Cain's house, and the warden would not release him from that obligation. He was one of the older prisoners, small in stature and not in very good health, probably due to the fact that he had been an alcoholic most of his life. He was a soft-spoken man, perhaps best described as meek.

Colonel Aucoin told me about a time a number of years back when Randy was granted a two-week furlough. This was when the department still allowed such things. According to the story, Randy returned to the rural community of Ruple, Louisiana, where he had been raised. When he arrived there, he could not locate a single member of his family. Even the house where they had lived had vanished. Since no one in the family could read or write, there had been no correspondence during all the years Randy had spent in prison. Just four days into his furlough, Randy returned to the prison. There was no other place for him to go.

Randy did not often speak in the group. When he did it was usually just to say how tired he was and how long and hard he had been working. When I questioned him once about how much he worked he said, "Every day." He explained that whenever one of Warden Cain's friends (usually from his church) wanted his or her garden put in or some special job done, the warden would send Randy to do it. This became such a regular occurrence that it often stretched his job out to seven days a week.

Working for Warden Cain had another disadvantage. It also meant that correctional officers would harass and taunt him about being the warden's "boy," assuming that special privileges came with the job. At one point, the harassment from the correctional officers in his dorm became so intemperate that others in the dorm began to complain about it in the community group. Randy, however, would not request to be transferred for fear that it would only exacerbate the problem with other officers.

Then, for a couple of weeks, Randy did not show up for the evening meetings, even though he had attended with regularity and seemed to enjoy them very much. Concerned, I asked Malcolm to check on him and see if he was all right. Malcolm's answer the next day left me very sad and angry. He said that when he returned to the dorm that night, he found Randy sitting on the side of his bunk exhausted and depressed. He began to weep as he quietly told Malcolm that the warden had been taking him to his home at night and putting him in a football uniform so that Warden Cain's thirteen-year-old son could use him for a tackle dummy.

I was told that things got so bad, even the associate warden, who lived next door to Warden Cain, felt sorry for Randy and offered to help him transfer to another prison. A few months later, Randy was transferred to a minimum-security facility in Baton Rouge. When Warden Cain realized what had happened, he had Randy returned to DCI within a week. This time, Randy was placed in a different unit, one from which he could not attend the drumming sessions. I never saw him again.

As the drumming sessions continued, we became more cautious. Toward the end of the sessions, before our time was up, I would remind the men, "When we finish tonight, you re-enter another world. You have to be careful, because this world and that world do not coexist. Your hearts are open now, but this prison is not a place to have an open heart."

I would hear the men remind each other, "Man, don't letcha self git stuck out 'dere, now," and then they'd leave the workshop with a sober demeanor.

In one of the subsequent sessions, I played a tape from the Buffalo Gap Conference in which Haki Madhubuti talked about racism in America. I will never forget the look on the face of the black correctional officer watching a white man sitting in a room talking about racism—and actually talking about white people's contribution to the epidemic of violence in this country. From that time on, word got around the prison to all the black correctional officers that I was an ally, a white man who was different. They also respected me for flooding the prison with books on African religion and culture that were written by African and African-American authors.

I called Haki Madhubuti. Not only was he an accomplished poet and author of a dozen books, but he also owned the publishing company Third World Press, two bookstores and a well-respected private school in south Chicago. I sent him a $500 check and asked him if would he choose some books that would be appropriate for our situation. Haki agreed and sent $1,000 worth of books.

When Haki's tape finished, one of the older prisoners, a huge black man nicknamed King Solomon, demonstrated a drumbeat and chant called *Hey Pakiway* that people played for the Indians at Mardi Gras. Some of the other men picked it up and began to play it on their drums. Then, one of the men, who had been a professional dancer, got up and started second-lining.

Second-line dancing is a New Orleans funeral tradition that has its roots in Africa. Grieving comes to completion as the procession marches to solemn music on the way to the grave. But as the family of the deceased turns away from the grave, they are also turning away from grief. The family then forms the first line of dancers, and the brigades of onlookers join in forming the second line. Accompanied by a marching band, this dancing allows the release of many emotions and it turns the rest of the funeral into a joyous celebration of life. The dance itself has no particular form except for struttin' to the beat with arms wavin', hips swingin' and legs high-steppin'.

More prisoners joined in, and soon everyone in the room was either dancing or drumming. When I stood up, I turned my hat sideways and began to dance with them. The room went wild. I happened to glance toward the correctional officer and found that he was up front drumming and singing "Hey Pakiway" along with the rest. That night, everyone in the room seemed to touch upon his song within, the one that each was born to sing. When all was quiet again, one of the men spoke bitterly that this would not last. Turning to me, he said, "The Man gon' kill this program and when 'dat happens, git these drums outa here." It was toward the end of this session that the prisoners for the first time referred to me as Brother. They even quipped that I was probably black. When time was up, I made sure to remind the men—especially the correctional officer—to be careful out there.

Underneath the joy of the workshops there was always a subtle current of sadness. Over the years, many of the prisoners had learned that nothing that caused them to feel joy and transformation could last, because those experiences were not allowed to happen in prison. The men felt this way for good reason. My workshops were becoming a threat because they had created a sense of respect and dignity among people who were, as Malcolm put it, "less than human" in the eyes of the administration. "Prisons are designed to break men's spirits, not to strengthen them," he said. Community building and drumming did the opposite. They built up men and helped them to truly grieve, heal and feel alive again. Men like Malcolm, who had years to go on their sentences and knew how the system worked, believed that they would still be there long after I and my program had been driven out.

As I continued to train Malcolm as a workshop facilitator, we were slowly becoming what Malcolm referred to as "the new odd couple." Malcolm had been my first and most steadfast ally at DCI and, as time went on, his insider's explanations of prison politics became crucial to the success of the program. Fearing that I would become labeled an inmate advocate, Malcolm warned me about standing up too often to the administration on behalf of the prisoners.

Although some of the correctional officers had begun to support our work, others began to covertly sabotage it as often as possible. Being thought of as an inmate advocate meant real danger for anyone who worked in a prison environment. I was told that one correctional officer who had previously refused to go along with the warden's program found his car riddled with pellets from a shotgun.

During the second year of our program, my assistant, Rusty, had to leave suddenly and was replaced by a man who was not familiar with the community-building process. At this point, Malcolm became an even more valuable asset in the workshops, as we added new dormitories to our program. One such workshop had gotten off to a disastrous start when correctional officers held the men at the sally port for over three hours in blistering heat.

At noon on the second day, I released the prisoners for lunch, turned to Malcolm and acknowledged my feelings of complete despair and hopelessness. "I'm lost, Malcolm," I said. "David is not able to help me, and I don't know how we're ever going to help this group to find its way into community." Malcolm's response left me astounded and relieved. "Bob, I think this group is right where it needs to be."

I knew immediately that he was right, and for the remainder of the workshop, I was able to let go of my anxiety, which the group was probably feeling as a pressure to "do the right thing." Later that day, Malcolm led the group down into its grief with a story about how he had recently apologized to his sister for all the trouble he had caused her in the past. I realized that Malcolm had learned to read the groups as well as I and at times better. It was also evident that Malcolm's presence was an important part of what made the workshops flow, in particular when the participants were new to the program and did not trust me, as the other prisoners who had come to know me did.

As our relationship continued to grow, I developed a deep knowing that Malcolm and I would be working together for a long time to come. "I don't know what it is," I told him, "but you and I have something important to do together." Having such a friend to watch my back meant a great deal to me. Even though I was trying to teach men about initiation, I was still new to the process and felt that my own initiation was far from complete. What Malcolm had to teach, I wanted to learn.

I knew too that, to many people, I looked like a fool. In the eyes of my family and friends, I was a person who had given up my marriage and a lucrative career in dentistry to work with "a bunch of criminals." In the eyes of the prison administration, I was a bleeding-heart liberal who was soft on the prisoners and all too often did strange things, such as drumming with the prisoners. Once, Warden Cain called me into his office and asked if I had become a guru. "Some of the security people told me that you have become a guru, and we don't need no gurus around here, Dr. Roberts." I assured the warden that I was far from being a guru. However, I was tempted to explain that if the prisoners were indeed using the term "guru," they were doing so out of respect; but I sensed that the warden would probably not understand.

In spite of the difficulties, by bringing concepts of community and the songs of Africa into the prison through books, drumming and the voices of Malidoma and Haki, I was, according to Malidoma, "bringing a certain light into the darkness of the prison." Recalling the time Malcolm told me that he had never felt an ounce of self-esteem until he had begun his study of Africa, I was encouraged to bring more material.

Malidoma warned me that I should be careful. Many who lived in the darkness would be jealous of the light and would try to steal it. Although this kind of light cannot be stolen, he explained, those who tried to could destroy it.

I had come to believe that becoming a man must include a willingness to look ridiculous in order to follow the commands of the soul. I also believed that true initiation creates transformations that are irreversible. For me, there could be no way of going back to my old ways of thinking.

In part, this conviction came from another lesson that Malidoma had taught me: We all come to this life from the spirit world for a purpose. On the journey here, however, we forget that purpose. In Malidoma's language, a word describing "initiation" more accurately translates into English as "remembering." He explained that Dagara initiation rituals are largely a process of remembering who a person is, what gift each person brings and what each one has come here to do.

By contrast, schools in the modern world tell only certain children that they are gifted. The others are thus led to believe that they did not come to this world with a gift. I knew this was true for me since I remembered being told at fourteen that I was "definitely not college material." I asked the prisoner groups if, like me, they had gotten this message from *their* teachers. All sadly nodded yes. As convincingly as I could, I told them that we had all been lied to—that it was a lie passed on through the pervasive ignorance of our culture.

Also, by contrast, Malidoma explained that the modern world has created an economy of scarcity, whereby certain commodities such as oil and foods become more valuable when they are in short supply. People exploit such an economy when they artificially deplete the supply of a commodity such as food and thereby artificially drive up its cost. The indigenous world, on the other hand, operates in an economy of abundance, where there is a constant giving and receiving of each person's gift. Malidoma told us that when Western anthropologists visiting his village commented about the incredible poverty they thought they saw, the villagers responded, "What poverty?"

Little by little, as I moved deeper and deeper into this work, I felt that I had finally "remembered" my own gift and my purpose. I had found the path I had been born to walk, and though terribly difficult, if I ever left it, I would become lost again. Although I was becoming more and more discouraged with the developments at the prison and the constant struggle to keep the program going, I knew I could never go back to the safe, comfortable life of privilege I had lived before. Since such transformations are irreversible, there would be no going home again, because *that* "home" no longer existed.

CHAPTER 5

Things Fall Apart

*T*here was a foreboding tension in Warden Cain's office as I entered that Thursday morning to talk about the upcoming week of literacy testing. The other two wardens and several correctional chiefs were with him, and they were talking about the work stoppage at Angola the previous day. That event was in all the newspapers and, even though they could restrict distribution of the newspapers in the prison, prisoners at DCI would surely hear about it.

The day before the work stoppage, one of Angola's maintenance crews had been assigned the task of building the state's new lethal injection table. One member of the job crew was understandably upset because his own brother had been executed in the same room the month before. Apparently, when this man refused to follow instructions, he was shackled and put into isolation after going through a place known to the prisoners as Red Hat. According to the stories I have heard, this place earned its nickname because when a prisoner emerged from there, his head was so bloodied that he looked as if he were wearing a red hat. To support this man, the remainder of his crew also refused and received the same consequences. As rumors of this story spread throughout the rest of the penitentiary, all other work crews joined in protest.

Back at DCI, Warden Cain was obviously concerned about the potential spread of the protest. The discussion ended when the warden gave instructions to serve the prisoners good food that day and make sure they got some watermelon. He followed his instructions with, "They'll do anything 'long as they get watermelon."

I had grown up hearing that expression. "A nigger'l do anything as long as you give him some watermelon." But I hadn't heard it in such a long time that I felt shaken to hear it again. Because it had disappeared from the circles I moved in, I naively believed it had disappeared completely. Moreover, I was appalled that this expression was imbedded in the prison administration's belief system to such an extent that it entered into the policies and practice of prison management.

As I heard this racist expression, I suddenly realized that the level of bigotry among these men was deeper than I had previously imagined. How deep did this extreme bigotry run within the department of corrections and throughout the state's criminal justice system? I had wanted to say something, because I didn't want my silence misconstrued as passive approval of the warden's language. If I had spoken out, however, such language would have simply gone into hiding, and that would put limits on what I still wanted to learn about the realities of prison life. I left the warden's office without further discussion.

We were now well into our second year of the program and about to test for reading skills improvement among the men of Dorm 1. My staff and I had recently decided that a full-time reading instructor would enhance our overall community program model. When the warden heard of this, he called me into his office. He told me that a woman at his Baptist church was looking for a job and would be ideal for this position. She was the wife of his church's choir director and a retired teacher. "What better qualifications can we find," the warden asked, "than a woman who can teach reading and quote the Scriptures at the same time?" I had serious concerns, but since I wanted to avoid having a discussion with the warden on a sensitive subject like religion, I agreed to interview his friend.

Needless to say, the warden's friend was not our choice for the job. But when I told this to my colleague at LSU who knew the warden, he emphatically warned me that I had better hire whomever the warden suggested. I took his advice under consideration, but I still knew that we had to hire someone who truly had the qualifications for this type of job. And who knows? If she could hold off quoting Scripture, she might be just the person we needed.

The retired teacher was a soft-spoken, middle-aged woman named Grace Hester. Her stated qualification was that she had taught at the junior high school level. It wasn't a surprise that Warden Cain decided to show up at her interview and began to tell her about the prison and how it was run. I was appalled at the words and convictions of this man, and even more so because he would state them so blatantly.

He told Grace, "What we have here is a slave camp. This is slavery. That's what hard labor is. All we care about here is that these men work. We don't care about them or their feelings or any of their concerns, only that they work."

Slavery! I thought. *Of course this is slavery. The prison even has the appearance of a plantation.*

When driving along the highway to DCI, the first thing one sees are the beautiful whitewashed wooden fences surrounding the green pastures that encircle the prison. In some fields there are black men hoeing crops and white men sitting on horseback, rifles at the ready. The administration building even looks like a large plantation house. It is painted white with a porch that extends completely around it. On the porch, facing the road, are rocking chairs, just as in the old days. Behind the main house there are the dormitories. In the antebellum period they would have been called slave quarters.

If Warden Cain's concept of incarceration was in fact one of slavery, then he must perceive the prisoners as slaves and perhaps himself as their master. As it turned out, however, he was using the term correctly. Later, I discovered that the term slavery remains, to this day, a part of the U.S. Constitution's Thirteenth Amendment. Even though that amendment supposedly abolished slavery forever, it left a significant exception:

> *Neither slavery nor involuntary servitude, except as a punishment for crime whereof the party shall have been duly convicted, shall exist within the United States, or any place subject to their jurisdiction.*
>
> U.S. CONSTITUTION, ART. 1, SEC. 1

Our Constitution makes the declaration that the enslavement of someone is morally acceptable, given the right circumstance. For this reason, one could say that the warden was correct in his usage of the term.

I did think, however, that such power is more power than any human being should have over another. I was reminded of Lord Acton's well-known axiom, "Power tends to *corrupt*; and absolute power *corrupts absolutely*." If he is correct, then how much closer can we come to absolute power than slavery? If our Constitution provides disproportionate power to this degree, we have to ask ourselves, is corruption actually *built* into our penal justice system?

In his exhaustive study in the late fifties and sixties, Karl Menninger described our overall system of corrections as an ineffective, expensive, barbarous and often law-breaking method of dealing with delinquency that only produces more delinquency. "I suspect that all the crimes committed by all the jailed criminals do not equal in total social damage that of the crimes committed against them," Menninger said.

Jerome Miller, commissioner of the Massachusetts Department of Youth Services, became the first (and only) American public official of the twentieth century to close down the reform schools of an entire state, dispersing delinquent youngsters to a broad spectrum of community programs. The current system of corrections in the United States "is probably the single greatest threat to our national well-being . . . [and] the single greatest contributor to crime and mayhem on the streets," Miller said. Researchers confirmed that the closures produced no serious increase in criminal behavior.

The most common example of institutional corruption that I learned about was drugs being sold in prison. I first heard of the problem from a patient of mine while I was still practicing dentistry. He had been convicted for forging a prescription for Percodan and spent several years at Angola. He came to see me upon his release from prison to replace several front teeth that had been knocked out in a fight while he was serving time. I had inquired about his addiction and how he was doing with his recovery process, and he said he was truly struggling to stay clean and had been on drugs the entire time he was incarcerated. Drugs, according to him, were much easier to obtain in prison than they had been on the street. He was not successful in his struggle and returned to prison within the year.

I have heard countless stories from men in prison and out of the substantial free flow of drugs in our jails and prisons, and I do not believe that visitors bring in more than a minuscule amount of the supply. In fact, twice during the period of research I conducted at DCI, correctional officers were caught smuggling contraband into the prison compound. I was told they had lost their jobs.

I have heard numerous accounts of an organization of drug dealers within the ranks of correctional officers at Angola at levels which include the top rank of colonel. Some of the stories have come from the men who themselves operated drug rings for correctional officers, and the stories were told to me by these men at a time when they had been released from prison and had nothing to gain by telling them. Without question, corruption is a major factor in our system.

My staff soon experienced Warden Cain's absolute power when we learned from LSU, which controlled our grant, that we were *expected* to hire his choir director's wife as our reading tutor. On her first day at the prison, we asked her to simply sit briefly with each group to get a feel for their reading acumen. I winced when I saw that she was sitting at a table with Robert Mole.

Robert was one of the most bizarre of all the people I had encountered at DCI. He was a drug addict who had financed his addiction by burglarizing homes. Nevertheless, he was also very intelligent, artistic and very intuitive. To this day, I have some of the drawings he gave me. Most are of mythological knights and demons, but sometimes he drew beautiful animals such as horses or wolves.

Robert often talked about his drug use as something he wanted to do, not something to which he was addicted. He loved to talk about smoking mushrooms and often drew pictures of them. He also enjoyed talking about his burglaries and the thrills he got from them. Addictions specialists know that the rush Robert got from his burglaries was part of his addictive process. What a kick it was for him to be walking down the street with his stolen goods and see a police car, siren screaming, rushing to the scene he had just left. He once bragged that while standing in a closet full of shoeboxes, he knew intuitively which one contained the hidden money. He told us that he always tried to pick an empty house, but that occasionally he slipped up and someone would be home. Sometimes he was in the house as the owners returned home, and he had to make a fast getaway. He ended up in prison only because he had been betrayed by a partner while fencing his goods.

On the surface, Robert Mole did not *seem* dangerous, and I'm still not sure if he really *was* dangerous at all. My intuition, however, was that there was a touch of sociopath in him. In the words of the poet Robert Bly, he appeared to have "lost his ability to shudder." In his life, the abnormal had become the normal—a denial so characteristic of addiction. I must add, however, that Robert Mole kept coming to our community workshops, and he was one of our most consistent and active participants when it came to speaking out in the group. It seemed to me that he wanted something out of the group, only he could never figure out how to get it. Remembering him saddens me.

Seeing him that morning sitting next to our new reading instructor, I became concerned about what Robert might choose to read to her. Among the many books that Haki Madhubuti had so generously sent us was the poetry of Ethridge Knight. His book, *The Essential Ethridge Knight*, which had won the 1987 American Book Award, was prison poetry. After being severely wounded in the Korean War, Ethridge had convalesced for a prolonged period of time in a veterans hospital in Indianapolis. There, he had become addicted to the recurrent doses of morphine. In time, he became a heroin addict, was arrested and sent to prison. As one might imagine, his poetry could be quite discomforting for some readers.

There was one poem in particular, titled "Feeling Fucked Up," that was written to describe the poet's feelings of immense loneliness when his woman walked out on him. In it, "fuck" appears a dozen times.

I was sure of two things. One was that Grace was not prepared for such poetry, and the second was that if Robert Mole saw *The Essential Ethridge Knight* on the table, he would go right to that poem. I scurried over to grab the book from the table, but I was too late. As I drew near, I saw the book in Robert's hands and heard Knight's words being read aloud to the choir director's wife.

> *fuck fanon nixon*
> *and malcolm fuck the revolution fuck freedom fuck*
> *the whole muthafucking thing*
> *all i want now is my woman back*
> *so my soul can sing.*

Grace did not appear to react, but I could only imagine her conversation with Warden Cain at church the next Sunday. After a few weeks, Grace found a new job.

In spite of all this, I tried to maintain my hopes for our future at DCI. Our interventions were working, and we were achieving dramatic and quantifiable results in reading scores and improved behaviors that other rehabilitation programs within the system were not.

A few weeks prior to the second barrage of testing in Dorm 1, though, disaster struck. Two of the initial workshop participants tested positive on a random drug screening. Both had been longtime trustees but were now remanded to medium-security status. This change took away the few privileges they had, privileges that dramatically improved the quality of their everyday lives. These two men worked on Crew 8, which cleaned the state capitol office buildings each day. The most prized benefit of this job was the opportunity to eat at one of the state cafeterias, where the food was considered to be of gourmet quality compared to prison food.

Both men had recently completed the parole process and were due to go home once their papers were in order. Instead, their paroles were officially revoked, meaning an additional two years imprisonment for one man and almost three for the other. Several of the men in their community group told me that the sergeant in charge of the men's work crew had given each of them a cold medication the night before. This was why they had tested positive. I investigated, since infractions were part of the data we collected and would affect the outcome of our study. The sergeant was very cooperative. He freely admitted that he commonly handed out cold medications when the men were sick so that he could keep his work crews at full force. This was so common a practice that the prisoners called him "the pharmacist." He even showed me the medication he was dispensing at the time.

I contacted the company who manufactured the drug test and asked for technical information about it. The toxicologist with whom I consulted just happened to be the man who had done most of the research that led to the development of the drug test DCI used. Regarding the cold medication the prisoners had been given, he said that it contained an ingredient called ephedrine, a compound common to some twenty-seven over-the-counter cold medications. The drug screening that had been used would give a positive result, he said, if any one of these twenty-seven non-narcotic medications was present in the urine. He then said, "I hope they are not taking any legal action against these men on the basis of this test, because it is only a screen, and was never intended to indicate conclusively the presence of an illicit drug. If that's what they have been doing, they are susceptible to a class-action suit against them, unless they are confirming the presence of illicit drugs with specific follow-up tests."

I knew that security had not been doing confirmation tests, and that for several years many legal (or illegal) sanctions that resulted in extended periods of imprisonment had been based solely on the screen test. Naively thinking that I was doing the warden a favor, even protecting him from a possible class-action lawsuit, I told him what I had discovered and I showed him the published literature the toxicologist had sent. The warden told me that it was too late to restore the men's parole dates, but that he would issue an order that they be restored to their trustee status. Though he thanked me, he did not say that legal sanctions taken as a result of this test would cease, and I was not certain how much he appreciated my report.

From this point on, I began to sense a growing hostility toward me from the administration. When the chief of security heard of my research into the drug-screening test, he confronted me on the yard. "You ain't gonna make me lose my drug test," he said angrily. My attempts to explain fell on deaf ears. Three years later, I learned the class-action lawsuit was being prepared against the department of corrections.

Until this time, I had not worried about interference from the prison staff getting too out of hand. I still had the secretary of corrections as a friend and powerful ally, and I knew I could call on him if and when it became necessary. I had not done so because I believed that I had sought the warden's input enough that he and I could work out any serious difficulties between us. I still believed that he would respect me more if I did not go over his head whenever I had a problem. Another reason I believed he would inevitably support our work was because he told me that his life's dream was to become famous, and he had high hopes that our program would inevitably accomplish this for him.

"Half of the harm that is done in this world," says the psychiatrist in T. S. Eliot's play *The Cocktail Party*, "is due to people who want to feel important. They don't mean to do harm, but the harm does not interest them, or they do not see it, or they justify it because they are absorbed in the endless struggle to think well of themselves."

———

A few months later, John Densmore called to say that he was speaking at Centenary College in Shreveport, Louisiana, and that he wanted to visit the drumming program at the prison. Although this was like a dream come true for me, it presented the problem of getting the men released from their duties for an afternoon. I reasoned, however, that having a famous person visit the prison would be consistent with Warden Cain's desire to someday become famous himself. To cover all my bases, I billed the gathering as including a motivational speech by John and a demonstration of drumming. John's wife, Leslie Neale, a lovely actress and brilliant filmmaker who was seven months pregnant at the time, accompanied him on the drive down from Shreveport. At first she told us that she did not intend to take part in the session. However, during our conversation at lunch she became convinced that being there would not only be safe but worthwhile and enjoyable.

When we entered the chapel where the meeting would be held, we saw that the men had already arranged the pews along the walls, removed the drums from their boxes and had begun playing. One of the members of the prison band had set up the band's trap set in the middle of the room for John. No introductions were necessary as we entered the room to the pulsations of drums. Someone immediately carried a conga drum over to John so he could join in. When the first sequence was finished, someone called the next rhythm's name, "Blood Brothers," and we all resumed playing for the next half hour. In the silence that followed, I finally introduced John and Leslie. Leslie's pregnancy and fair hair, together with her compassion, brightness and beauty, brought an extraordinary and hopeful feminine energy into the room. I asked John if he would like to say a few words, unaware that he had become filled with emotion and could hardly speak. With eyes moistened, he choked out the words, "I love you," to the roomful of men and we continued the drumming again, huddled together for a while longer in a soulful exaltation of rhythms.

John eventually moved to the middle of the room and played along on the trap set to "Haitian Hypnotique," a beat from the Caribbean, followed by "Manjani," the beat Aidoo had taught us. One of the men there, the leader of the prison band, was a very talented musician from New Orleans who had lost control of his life because of his drug addiction. He asked the group's permission to "bring a little jazz onto the scene" by adding his trumpet to the mixture of rhythms. This, of course, brought on the second-line dancers from New Orleans. For a while, anyone who was not playing a drum or some other rhythm instrument was up dancing. This included Rosie, John and myself. The final beat of the day was the *Ibo* beat from Africa in which everyone shouted "Ibo!" during the pause at the end of each segment. After a short time, I realized that everyone had begun to shout "Solo!," in hopes of persuading John to play a drum solo on the traps. When he finally heard their cry, he responded with a staggering, mind-blowing drum solo. The men could hardly contain the passion that John's talent and spirit brought into that room. On his signal at the end of the solo, the group once again took up the *Ibo* beat and played until our time was almost over. The silence at the end of the beat lasted about three minutes and had the same quality of soulful intensity that began each of our community-building sessions.

One of the prisoners, Herman Tasker, broke the silence with an expression of gratitude to John and Leslie for their generosity and compassion. He told them how the drumming and African studies sessions had helped him to let go of the shame he had felt since his youth about being black. He said that even being elected president of his senior class in high school had not removed the stigma he felt.

He told how his shame had deepened into despair over his

parents' suicides, which he had never talked about until he joined the community-building sessions with Rosie and me. "When alcohol could no longer cover up the shame," he said, "I turned to heroin. I hope now that, without all that shame, I can live without the drugs."

Clarence Williams closed the session with a soulful African grief chant that I had taught the group a few weeks before. "Pourdhah Sominée, Pourdhah Mominée" honors grandfathers and grandmothers and ends with a raspy "Rhah!," which engenders the memory of the sound a small child makes when leaping into the lap of a grandparent.

John and Leslie were obviously moved. On the way back to the airport, they spoke in earnest of somehow telling the world about the human kindness, dignity and respect they had just witnessed from men whom much of the world perceived as garbage. Leslie, who was already an accomplished documentary filmmaker, said that we must try to capture these stories on film and show how wrong such perceptions are. She promised that she would work toward that end. Eventually, her promise resulted in the documentary film *Road to Return*, which is about the ravages of prison life and its debilitating effects on one's chances of survival on the outside. The film featured an interview with Sister Helen Prejean, author of *Dead Man Walking*, and narration by the actor Tim Robbins. All the stories the men and women tell in the film end with a common statement, "I've never told this to anyone."

Before we could get the necessary clearances to begin that task, however, disaster struck a second time, and it was the second disaster in what would become a long string of disasters. Louisiana Governor Charles Roemer, the man who had granted me the opportunity to conduct this research, lost his bid for a second term to the former governor, Edwin Edwards, whom he had unseated four years earlier. In my opinion, this was the strangest and most tragic election in the history of Louisiana.

Governor Roemer miscalculated his support and he ran a weak campaign that cost him a place in the runoff election, but, even more unfortunate, racism had once again raised its ugly head high enough to propel Ku Klux Klan Grand Wizard David Duke into a runoff with the flamboyant and corrupt Edwards, who would later be convicted on seven felony counts in federal court. An alleged crook or a bigot—that was our choice. When Edwards took office again, the first cabinet position to be replaced was the only person who could protect us if we were ever to need it—our ally, Secretary of Corrections Bruce Lynn.

A few weeks after the inauguration, Rosie and I arrived at the prison on the morning we were to give the literacy posttest for the second round of experimental test groups. We had spent the past three months evaluating our previous data and repeating the exact process we employed with Dorms 7, A and B. Scientific proof requires not only that an intervention be effective, but also that its effectiveness be demonstrated repeatedly. So this second round was vital to one of our hypotheses: that community building could make a significant difference in the outcome of a prison literacy program.

Accordingly, we had randomly selected three additional dormitories, led one of them through a very successful community-building workshop and then followed up with seven weeks of literacy training for all three groups. Our plan was to measure the improvement in their reading scores when compared to their pretests. We were horrified when only a handful of the participants in the community-building group showed up for the test. Those who did said that they had been awakened at ten the night before and told to remove their belongings from their footlockers and prepare to move to another dormitory. They spent the entire night being scattered from place to place by the night crew and they had not been allowed to sleep. The remainder of the community group had been conscripted into the work detail that morning at the crawfish plant. Over three months of formidable and expensive research had been summarily destroyed. Rescheduling the tests was not an option since the delicate spirit of community, which brought about the mutual support of each person for the other, had been shattered by the permanent scattering of the group to other dormitories.

This time, I went to the warden's office to protest. He claimed ignorance but told me that the correctional officers were obviously sabotaging the program because I had "taken sides with the two prisoners in the drug-testing incident." He apologized (sincerely, I thought) and promised me that he would do whatever he could to make sure that this never happened again. In spite of this promise, a ranking correctional officer who saw the value of our work warned me that I had to be careful because many of the correctional officers now considered me an inmate advocate.

This marked the beginning of overt sabotage to the community-building, literacy and cultural workshops. The workshop participants began to report stories of harassment and threats from the correctional officers should they continue to attend the sessions. One group that ate early, in order to make it to the community session on time, was reprimanded and written up for eating out of turn. Those who waited their turn received write-ups for being late for the call out. Others who had some of the preferred jobs in the prison were told by their supervisors that they would lose those jobs if they missed work by going to a program.

Eventually, it became difficult for us to maintain attendance at the reading and community sessions. The whole world seemed to be walking backward. Prisoners who did not know how to read and were being offered the fastest track ever to escape their illiteracy were having to turn down this opportunity. However, we understood their reluctance. Some of them had years to go on their sentences.

When our work was done at the prison and we were gone, how would they fare?

Soon after, the administration announced that it needed the office space we had occupied for the past year. This left us with no place to work and no phone, and I had to keep all of our records, our typewriter and our supplies in the trunk of my car.

Even though I had lost much of my naiveté, I was still taken aback by these developments. How could prison administrators and correctional officers, people who were sworn to uphold the law and safeguard the public safety, overtly sabotage an effort that demonstrated such potential for breaking the ever-growing cycle of drugs, violence, crime and imprisonment? Here, in the very place where they worked, they had witnessed a dramatic reduction in violence and all other rule infractions. In fact, the correctional officers hired to monitor the dormitories requested community dorms as their assignment because of the respect they received there. Furthermore, how could these individuals get away with sabotaging our program? This was supposed to be law enforcement.

The men in the program were not as naive as I was, and none of this surprised them. They had predicted from the first that this program would not last, but I had not believed them. During one of the drumming sessions, the men warned me again to get the drums out of the prison so they would not be confiscated. My disbelief was waning.

The next major disaster struck four months later on the morning of the literacy test for the third group. Only a fraction of the men showed up, because they had again been kept awake all night and then sent elsewhere on work details. When I went to the warden to protest and to remind him of his promise, he said, "Oops, we forgot."

Then the final blow occurred. During one of the ongoing community-building sessions with Dorm 7, the door suddenly burst open and a correctional officer announced that Warden Cain wanted to see me in his office. I responded that I would be there as soon as the current session ended. A few minutes later, the officer returned and said that the warden wanted to see me right away. Reluctant but worried, I closed down the group and went to the warden's office. At the conference table sat the warden, his two assistant wardens and Colonel Aucoin, who had covertly been our only ally among the staff and who had recently become the first black chief of security at the prison. In addition, there sat the professor whom I knew from the department at LSU that hosted our study and administered our grant, the same professor who had originally talked me into taking the study to DCI, where he was a long-time, personal friend of the warden. On several occasions, he had asked me to let him use some of the money in our grant for departmental purposes—primarily for travel. I had refused him. As a federal grantee, we were responsible to justify every cent we used. Still, I continued to trust him and to follow his advice on academic matters until, in a conversation one day, he began to refer to the prisoners as niggers. From that point, I knew this man had nothing to teach me and, gradually, I ended all contact with him. That is, until this meeting.

This professor announced that I was being removed as principle investigator of the grant and that he was taking over. In addition, my salary was being cut by 30 percent and my travel benefits were eliminated. This meant that the costs of our weekly commutes to the prison and lodging expenses would have to come out of our own pockets.

My blood began to boil, and I could feel my soul wanting to leap out of my body and choke off what this man was saying. Barely able to remain in my seat, I asked for an explanation. I was told that I had "mishandled" some of the grant funds with which we operated the study. Without thinking, I said, "You know as well as I do that's a lie."

Then the strangest thing of all happened. The professor got out of his chair and started toward me. My mind raced. I suddenly remembered the time when one of the prisoners left his seat and walked across the circle yelling at me because I had not answered his question. He had stopped about six feet in front of me and shouted every four-letter word I had ever heard in my life. I remained still except for gently nodding my head to encourage him to get all of his rage out of his body so that he could fully participate in the workshop. When he had done just that, he walked calmly back to his seat, sat down and began to laugh in a manner that was in no way disrespectful. I told the group, "That's where our joy always lies hidden—underneath our rage."

The strategy did not work this time. My former friend kept moving toward me, and suddenly I saw his fist coming. Since I had waited too long to stand up, my only option was to lean back to avoid his blow. Fortunately, the chair was the recliner type, and it allowed me enough movement to get out of the way. But in missing his mark the professor lost his balance, fell on top of me and toppled my chair backward, sending us both crashing to the floor. The next face I saw was that of Colonel Aucoin as he was pulling the professor off of me. As I leaped up, one of the assistant wardens, Bubba McNeil, grabbed me and shoved me against the wall. I had always intuitively believed that Warden McNeil was an even stronger covert ally to our efforts than Daniel. Sure enough, under the noise and fury of the moment, I heard him whisper, "Don't do nothin'." I answered quickly, "Okay."

As I felt Bubba relax his hold, I knew in an instant that this had been a set up to get rid of me altogether. I also knew that Bubba had figured I might strike back, and he was protecting me from falling deeper into their trap. Later, Daniel verified my suspicions. To this day, I am deeply grateful to these two men who risked their own well-being for mine.

I met Rosie in the visiting hall and told her what had happened. We did not know what to do, but we wanted to get

the hell out of there and never come back. Reality inter-
vened, however, and although we were potentially facing further hostility if we remained, we knew that leaving would
mean we could not complete our research and publish the
results that the men had worked so hard and taken such risks
to achieve. Everything we had *all* worked for would be lost.
That evening, we decided to allow a few days to pass to see if
things had cooled down enough so we could finish our task.

———

The following day when we arrived at the prison, I immediately found Malcolm at his job in the kitchen and told him
what had happened. He had already heard from some of the
black correctional officers who attended our drumming sessions that there might be a plan to plant illicit drugs in the
trunk of my car and in his footlocker. Later, as I passed
Colonel Aucoin's office, he signaled me to come in and he
closed the door behind us. He told me that from then on, he
wanted me to park my car just outside his window, just a few
yards away from the spot where Perry Bernard carried on his
daily job of washing cars. Daniel said that he and Perry would
try to keep us safe for whatever time we had left at the prison.
    At this juncture, I reluctantly concluded that neither
community building, nor any other serious treatment program could, in the long run, succeed at DCI or any other

prison like it. This was not because of the prisoners. It was because of unequivocal sabotage by the very people who could have received the most immediate benefits of greater ease in prison management.

In spite of the project's astonishing success in reducing violence and increasing literacy levels, the administration made good on its plan, and I was officially removed as head of the program. Watching over two years of research being eroded by the very people who should have been giving us their support, and uncertain of what the future would bring, I knew only one thing for sure: DCI was no longer a safe place for me or for Malcolm.

In the following weeks at the prison, Rosie and I became nonpeople. We were not asked to attend any meetings, and we were allowed only to continue the ongoing community sessions we had already begun. Fortunately, I was still able to collect information and data on infractions and the like that demonstrated the effectiveness of our interventions.

Since the correctional officers at the sally ports were accustomed to seeing me walk in and out carrying drums, I began to take one or two drums a week out of the prison to store them at home. I advised John Densmore of our situation and of what the men had said about getting the drums out. He offered to write a letter expressing his wishes that the drums continue to be a part of whatever program I conducted in the future. I continued to carry the drums out late in the afternoons when it was dark and the warden and his staff had gone home for the day. Fortunately, we had kept the large boxes in which the drums were shipped, and we had continued to store them there after each session. So whenever anyone entered the large room, they saw the same stack of boxes they had always seen. Except each week, more of them were empty.

In spite of the shadow cast over the whole program, the community sessions continued to teach and transform me. In one of the last Dorm 7 sessions, I noticed that Malcolm was on Perry's case, but in a friendly manner. Perry, on the other hand, seemed more somber. Most of the time, there was a verbal jousting that went on among the prisoners, although I had never been quite sure how to interpret its true meaning. In the warehouse where I worked as a teenager, my black coworkers used to keep this same unending tournament of words, known as "playin' the dozens," going between themselves. It seemed to offer them a way to play and yet remain serious, masculine and strong. It had a quality of keeping their swords, as verbal skills, sharpened. Often, a given verbal match would come to a point where there was suddenly a clear winner. The vanquished opponent, with nothing left to counter, would offer his touché, saying, "Okay, you got that one," and the contest would begin again. A prisoner once told me that black men had developed this practice as a viable defense mechanism with which to outwit the white man when necessary, and it offered less potential for landing the "swordsman" in jail. In its less serious mode, this bantering often held much humor and charm. In silence I would experience its humor, and I would sometimes be amazed at the deftness of accomplished and discerning masters.

Malcolm was for the most part too serious to practice this joust, but when he did, he seemed always to retain an aura of respect for himself and his opponent. While bantering with Perry today, however, his style seemed slightly different, though I could not discern why.

The theme of that day's group soon became apparent as one story after another dwelt on the men's fathers. One man who had not spoken to his father in seven years told us that his father had cancer. Another told about the day his father had committed suicide. Charles Middlebrooks said, mournfully, that he had no idea who his father was and had not understood until this day that it mattered.

Bubba Sanders came in late and apologized for his late arrival. Right away, everyone noticed that he had just shaved his head. I tried not to look shocked. Though Bubba was big, well built and handsome, the difference made him look absolutely crazy to me. I said nothing and smiled when he quipped with the group about it.

A few months before, Bubba had announced that he was getting married. He had somehow reconnected with an old acquaintance who was recovering from a cocaine addiction while trying to raise four children. Many of the guys had tried to talk Bubba out of the marriage, but to no avail. I simply asked him if he felt okay about the simultaneous prospects of a new marriage, four kids and his own difficult recovery. I did not argue when he said yes. Instead, I tried to understand how important it was for someone in prison to feel a part of the outside world and the effect marriage could have on one's sense of belonging.

Bubba talked about his new wife, his wedding and how his family had tried to talk him out of it. He was very disturbed to learn from his bride that the prison was returning her mail to him stamped "no prisoner here by that name." He sounded confused when he spoke about becoming the stepfather of four young boys. "For one thing, I don't even know why I got married. And, besides that, I don't even know if I can talk to them." He said that his awkwardness kept him from saying much to the boys at the wedding. There was a brief silence. The next week, Bubba said he had called his new wife and another man answered the phone. He was asking how one goes about getting a divorce from a prison cell. Fortunately, she was willing to do it.

He told us about his growing fear of leaving prison as his parole hearing approached. He recalled that he had spent so little time in the outside world that it was like something he had once dreamed about. Bubba feared his strength would not be enough to stay off drugs. He identified with the fears Malcolm had expressed in an earlier session, that there would be a crucial time when he would need his full wits about him—and he feared that prison had damaged or weakened them.

The group became quiet again. We had about fifteen minutes left. I considered that perhaps the men had gone as deep as they could for the day. I paused, then spoke about the profound feeling of community that I had experienced with them and praised them for the openness and respect they had given each other.

Then Perry said, "Ya'll hold up a minute. I been sorta holding back an' I want to talk about something." As he began to talk about *his* deceased father, how much he had loved him and how his father had always given him advice, his eyes moistened and his voiced became choked, "And, he . . ." He pointed to Malcolm and wept openly. When he could talk again, he told us how Malcolm reminded him of his father and always gave him good moral advice. "He even looks like him," he said with a catch in his voice. He then began sobbing.

I could see that Bubba, sitting next to Perry, was deeply stirred. He placed his hand on Perry's shoulder and stroked him a bit. I sat and stared, taking in this beautiful sight of love and concern of one man for another, a black man and a white man. I thought, *If only the different races in the ordinary world could become this close and connect at this level, what a different place it could be. What a distorted image the world has of men in prison.*

Malcolm said, "I realize now why I've been hard on you lately." Reminding us that Perry had his parole date and would be leaving soon, he continued. "Once again, as I swear every time I will not do, I have allowed myself to love someone who will leave me behind, and I know I've been unconsciously separating myself from you." He apologized to Perry.

I paused again. We had now run a bit over time. We stood in a silent circle and hugged one another. When the session ended, I walked with Bubba back to the main compound and asked him about his shaved head. He explained that the correctional officers often harassed him for his unusually short temper, knowing they could get a rise out of him. "Once," he said, "they came to take away my radio, for no reason. So, rather than give it to 'em, I just smashed it on the floor, an' they threw me in the dungeon.

"But if they think someone is crazy," he said, "or about to really blow off, they're scared of him an' they'll leave him alone. An', you know, I been doin' a lot a thinkin' lately about my life since I been comin' to community, an' I just need them to leave me alone right now. So I shaved my head so I'd look crazy an' they'd fur sure leave me alone."

A few weeks later, Bubba was granted parole. Suddenly, it began to dawn on me how attached to him I had become. I could not help thinking of how distressed I would be if he were one of my own sons going back out into the world as unprepared as he was. "The outside world was like a dream," he had said. To me, he was like a wild pup raised in captivity, about to be returned to nature without having learned the skills of survival. Everyone knows we cannot do that with animals, and yet we turn out "pups" from prisons every day, young men who have served what is called "juvenile life." Juvenile life, in most states, refers to a sentence in which a juvenile spends the remainder of his youth incarcerated until the age of twenty-one. Also in most states, he is transferred to an adult facility where he spends the last three years of his juvenile life. These young men did not have the right skills when they went into prison, and they have no new learned skills when they get out.

The mandatory sentencing laws of the nineties are increasing this problem by geometric proportions. Mandatory sentencing laws dictate the minimum length of sentence for any given crime, thus removing much discretion from judges in each case he/she tries. A perfect example is Perry Bernard's youngest sister, who is presently serving three life sentences for her conviction as a drug dealer. It is important to note that she is a first-time, nonviolent offender caught up in the federal government's knee-jerk reaction to the bogus "crack epidemic." Such laws have been a major contributor to prison overcrowding because the correctional system loses its ability to control prison populations.

Bubba had served juvenile life when he was younger, and of course, he wound up back in prison. Now, we were throwing him back into the river again, and we expected him to know how to swim. I gave him some clothing, a little money and was able to arrange for him to live at a place called Hope House, a halfway house of sorts operated by a Catholic charity in Baton Rouge. He could remain there for only six months, but it was the best I could do for him at the time. I told him I hoped he would immediately find an Alcoholics Anonymous group, obtain a sponsor and stay in touch with me. However, within months, he was back in jail on charges of possession and use of marijuana.

Malcolm was the next to leave DCI. One of the women who ran the kitchen in Malcolm's unit was married to a department of corrections sergeant at a facility in Baton Rouge known as the Police Barracks. Aware that DCI had become unsafe for Malcolm, she persuaded her husband to arrange for his transfer. The Police Barracks was a small minimum-security facility at the state police headquarters from which the prisoners would go out to various state buildings to work. Malcolm was assigned as a cook in the cafeteria of the nearby state police training academy.

Though I felt tremendous relief seeing him out of DCI, I knew that without the inside information he always provided, Rosie and I were more vulnerable to the corrupt ways of our prison hosts. Thankfully, Colonel Aucoin had replaced Perry in the wash bay with another prisoner whom we could trust to watch my car.

Some good news did finally arrive. My dissertation committee had been so impressed with the findings thus far in our research that they enthusiastically accepted my defense of it and allowed me to graduate with my Ph.D. in curriculum and instruction, after seven years of struggle.

I had previously written a theoretical dissertation about group processes that included community building. The writing, for me, would remain completely without soul, however, until I was able to include an actual experiment with community building and demonstrate its effects empirically. When portions of it were accepted for publication in the *Journal of Offender Rehabilitation*, Dr. Earl Cheek, department chair and chair of my committee, asked that I include his name on it. He has since told me that he now requires all his Ph.D. candidates to read my dissertation before beginning theirs.

In light of all the disasters at the prison, my graduation was a welcomed opportunity to celebrate. Rosie and I had been depressed upon seeing our program destroyed. We were certain that our positions would soon be terminated, and there was no one at the prison able to continue the workshops, even though the administration said they planned to. Not since my years in the warehouse had my future seemed so uncertain and my life so confused. At least, I felt, my new Ph.D. would hold out some promise of future employment in my chosen field. I couldn't return to dentistry. I felt that doing so would have been like climbing aboard a sinking ship. It was not even a practical idea since I no longer had any instruments, patients nor the collateral required to take out a massive loan to set up a new office.

Besides, at that point, I had no desire to remain in Louisiana or even the South. The racial bigotry and hatred I had just experienced among the same kind of people I had grown up around left me with a sickness so serious that I did not think I could recover in the same corner of the world in which I had contracted it.

My greatest confusion swirled around the question of who I was now and why I was on this earth. I felt that community building was for me like the gift that Malidoma said each of us brings from the spirit world—the means by which we can fulfill our purpose for coming to this life. However, if, in my work with prisoners, I had remembered the path I came here to walk, it now felt as if someone had dropped a bomb on it.

*

I must have sent out a hundred résumés during those weeks of pondering my future, and I never received a single response. I even tried to get a job teaching high school and was turned down because I had no teaching certificate.

Then the letter Rosie and I anticipated arrived. Our work at the prison would be terminated within three weeks. There was one hidden blessing, however. Joan Thompson, who headed the human resources department at the university, had been very supportive of our project by helping us through the massive, complicated administrative processes that a state university can generate. We had, on occasion, related to her some of the stories we collected from the prison. She said they inspired her and left her feeling hopeful. When we told her of our circumstance, she said that since we were terminated, as opposed to having the positions themselves eliminated, we would be eligible for unemployment benefits. It afforded each of us only $180 per week, but it sure beat nothing. Had the professor known about this, we were certain he would have terminated the positions, since the money for our unemployment checks came directly out of what were now *his* grant funds.

In our last days at the prison, we took our groups through closure and said our good-byes. We were satisfied that at least we had learned something new and important (or perhaps we remembered something ancient and forgotten) and that the knowledge had tremendous potential to make a remarkable difference in the world of criminal justice. We just had no idea what to do with this hard-earned knowledge. On our very last day, Colonel Aucoin asked me to stop by his office. When I arrived, he looked up from his desk and handed me the following weekend's extra-duty list. These were the men who the week before had committed some minor infraction and were now receiving punishment for it. There were eight names on it, none of which I recognized. They would have to work the weekend at some menial job, such as cutting grass with a swing blade. It also meant that they could have no visitors during this time.

He said, "I got this list this morning and thought about what a difference you've made here. Knowing this was your last day, I had my secretary find me the extra-duty list from the week you arrived. Back then, there were *eighty-eight* names on that list. You did this," he said, "you and your program." I thanked him for protecting us during the past few months, and I said I hoped that our paths would cross again.

I then got word that the associate warden, Kelly Ward, wished to see me in his office. He leaned back in his chair as I entered and said that he wanted to clarify that the drums that had been donated to the project would remain the property of the prison. I showed him the letter John Densmore had sent and told him that I intended to take them with me to use in whatever program I did next. I did not tell him they were all sitting in my living room, bedrooms and staircase, except for one that was in the trunk of my car. All of the drum boxes in the storage room were empty. He said he didn't think that I would be allowed to remove the drums, but that we could take up the issue with the warden when he returned the following week. I agreed and walked out, then returned to leave him with a copy of John Densmore's letter.

Rosie and I spent the next weeks sending out résumés and searching the classified ads for jobs. Once a week, we had to go down to the unemployment office to sign for our $180 and fill out a declaration that we were looking for work. I had a couple of interviews, one at Marquette University in Milwaukee and one at the Medical School of Wisconsin, but to no avail. Then Rosie got lucky. Harry Connick, the district attorney of New Orleans and father of the well-known singer Harry Connick Jr., wanted to begin a program called Diversion, in which first-time, nonviolent drug offenders could avoid prosecution by entering six months of drug treatment. With her background, credentials and recent experience with offenders at DCI, Rosie was their unquestionable first choice. So, after only six weeks of unemployment, we had one salary coming in again, albeit a small one.

Since Rosie was now our breadwinner, I took on the job of househusband. I had enjoyed cooking since attending a three-week French cooking school nine years earlier, at age forty. Cooking was my only source of joy, however. Most of the time, I was consumed by dark inner feelings of grief, anger, rage and hatred about what had occurred and, of course, by fear about the future. What little savings we had was rapidly dwindling, and I still had no prospects for a job.

On occasion during those weeks of confusion, I drove up to Baton Rouge to see Malcolm. He had, of course, become well respected at the Police Barracks, which made my visiting requests easy to arrange. Over time, I became acquainted with the assistant director of that facility, who was always searching for prisoners who could be trusted in a minimum-security setting. On my recommendation, Danny Dunn and Clarence Williams were transferred from Dorm 7 at DCI to this facility, which allowed the four of us to reminisce about the community we loved so well.

One evening during our conversation, Malcolm said that one question about me still remained within his heart. But he would not tell me what it was. My curiosity was rewarded only with a promise that someday he would tell me. That day finally came several months later.

In the meantime, I had begun to imagine that if community building could be so effective at the prison, in spite of the system's hostility, how much more successful could a program be that worked with former prisoners who were out on the street? Without question, they would struggle with the same issues they had to deal with on the inside, including the challenge of survival. I imagined how the components of our earlier work could be greatly expanded to include education in basic computer skills, drug treatment, family involvement, employability training and job placement. Classes in these vital areas could be offered and the community-building component would enhance them, just as it had enhanced the reading skills of the men at DCI. And, in the best of all worlds, I could operate the program in complete independence from the correctional system. Great idea! But who would fund it? In the meantime, I continued to look for a job.

CHAPTER

6

Confusion and Despair

Oh my friends,

What can you tell me of Love,

Whose pathways are filled with strangeness?

When you offer the Great One your love,

At the first step your body is crushed.

Next be ready to offer your head as his seat.

Be ready to orbit his lamp like a moth giving in to the light,

To live in the deer as she runs toward the hunter's call,

In the partridge that swallows hot coals for love of the moon,

In the fish that, kept from the sea, happily dies.

Like a bee trapped for life in the closing of the sweet flower,

Mira has offered herself to her Lord.

She says, the single Lotus will swallow you whole.

Mirabai[5]
c. 1498–1546
Translated by Robert Bly

Over the following weeks I continued to send out résumés and search the classifieds for jobs. In the meantime, I made my weekly sojourn down to the unemployment office for my $180 check. Then, I heard from a friend in my hometown that the position of dean of student affairs was opening up at Shreveport's LSU Medical School. I felt I could do well in such a job and, since I knew both the chancellor and the current dean of student affairs, perhaps a door was opening— maybe it was even my next calling. What was more, if this were my path, it would locate me closer to my two youngest sons, who were still in school in Shreveport, and put me closer to the friends I had left behind.

I immediately drove up to Shreveport only to find, upon visiting my friend who was leaving the position, that another faculty member had decided to take the job. The voices from the past that said I was crazy to walk out on my career and family to work in a prison returned. Those voices had never completely gone away, but now they were shouting, "What is all this crap about a calling and a path to walk? You're a dentist who walked away from a perfect life on some quest to change the world and nearly got his nuts shot off."

There were times I was almost consumed by the grief and rage I felt. I also spent much time reflecting on my own mistakes, searching for accountability, second-guessing how I could have done things better or even perhaps pulled the whole thing off. Part of my anger and grief was for the men whom I had left behind at DCI, black men who had spent their lives hating white people, but in the end, had called me their brother.

—⸺⸺—

Nine months earlier, I had begun a campaign to win Malcolm his freedom. He had already completed the long three-year process of applying for a pardon and had won approval from the state pardon board. All that remained was for the governor to sign it. As Governor Roemer was leaving office, both Bruce Lynn and I had contacted him about signing the document before he left office, and he had agreed to look into it. I felt such confidence that the combination of Malcolm's record, the secretary of corrections' support and my efforts would show him worthy of a pardon.

On his last day of office, however, the governor still had not signed the pardon, and our hopes were lost. When word of this circulated throughout DCI, the entire prison mourned. Malcolm was so highly regarded by the other prisoners that many of them were saying, "If [Malcolm] Hill can't get a pardon, what hope is there for me?" At this time, he had served twelve years of his original twenty-five year sentence. The news was even more disheartening when I heard that a white man who had served only seven years for brutally beating his wife to death during a drunken stupor had recently been paroled. After killing her, he threw her body onto the bed of his pickup truck and drove to the local hospital where, according to witnesses, he grabbed her by her bloody hair and slung her onto the emergency room floor and left. When the warden found out that this man was a heavy equipment operator, he rented a bulldozer (at the state's expense) and had this prisoner build a lake across the road from the prison. Afterward, according to the story, the pardon board made this man eligible for parole, and he was soon released.

One of the benefits of Malcolm's transfer to the Police Barracks in Baton Rouge was that it looked good on a prisoner's record. This meant that pardon and parole applications were more likely to be granted. Even this, however, turned out to be a mixed blessing. I felt great relief that he was out of danger from those who saw him as a threat at DCI. Then his letters to me began to take on a more and more desperate tone. Malcolm wrote that the agony of coming so close to freedom was prolonged and intensified by living so close to freedom every day and knowing he was not free. At the Police Barracks, there were no fences and a prisoner could walk all the way to the curb of the street, but he could not step off. Everyday, there were constant, tantalizing reminders of the outside world, such as seeing families driving down the street in their cars. While most people take such things for granted, for a man who has been incarcerated for twelve years in a high-security prison, the sight, smells and experiences of the outside world bring with them an almost overwhelming longing to just "step off the curb" and leave. I promised Malcolm that I would redouble my efforts and, somehow, get the new governor, Edwin Edwards, to sign his pardon. Meanwhile, my vision of a community-building program with former prisoners continued to grow stronger.

While I kept looking for a job, I decided to call an old friend who had been a fraternity brother in my undergraduate days. Mike Sport had become very wealthy in the oil business in New Orleans, and I thought he might have some advice as to where I should look for funding. He told me that he was a member of the New Orleans Business Council, which at times offered seed money for innovative ideas that addressed local issues such as crime prevention. From a private list of members, he gave me the phone number of Bob Howsen, the current council chairman and CEO of a $2.6 billion per year corporation. Three calls to him over the following two weeks, however, yielded nothing beyond promises from his secretary.

Hence, in spite of my dreams, prayers and meditations, my despair and confusion continued to grow. Though I had believed with all my heart that I had been called to that work at DCI, I was now regressing into a *need* to believe this. Otherwise, I told myself, I had been a complete fool, and my financial situation offered me daily encouragement to believe just that. If I had a spiritual path to follow, what the hell had happened to it? I also pondered Malidoma's words about the gift each soul brings to offer to the village. Did I just want to believe it was true, or was it really true? I decided to contact him or go see him, in hopes of finding some direction or at least some encouragement to hang onto my dreams. If I did not find what I needed, I would begin my journey back to my old life and attempt to salvage my career in dentistry.

———

I had saved a brochure that had come some months earlier that said that the following November, Malidoma was to teach at another Multicultural Men's Conference, this one in Virginia. It was already October and I had not planned to go because of the cost. Now, however, I had reached a major crossroads and was in dreadful need of trusted guidance before choosing my direction. The conference organizer remembered me from the previous conference and was kind enough to give me a scholarship. Malcolm expressed his happiness for me that I would be able to again have counsel with Malidoma, but we both sadly remembered our dream of his pardon being signed and the two of us meeting Malidoma together.

Arriving at the conference, I decided to wait until I could catch Malidoma alone to discuss my questions. Until then, I would just participate in the scheduled program. The gathering began, like the other Men's Conferences, with the expressions of brokenness and grief. The men shared several stories about sexual abuse between mother and son, stories that had a profound impact on me. I had never before in my life heard of such a thing. If this had happened to someone in the prison project, it had not come to light.

At last, after three long nights of community building, Malidoma offered to teach us a ritual that would finish the job of purging this grief from the body. Following the ritual, the next morning was filled with brilliant lectures from James Hillman, Haki Madhubuti and Malidoma. In the afternoon, more stories began to surface from even deeper places, and we decided to repeat the ritual that evening. Within the group, I recounted the events of the prison project and its sad demise. During the ritual, which continued into the early hours of the next morning, I felt my grief and rage leave my body, and I felt lighter, as though grief and rage had mass and weight.

Exhausted when the ritual was over, my four roommates and I returned to our cabin, but we could not end the conversations about this combined process of community building and ritual. Then, and I do not remember why, someone pulled out a book of poetry, and soon we were reciting poetry, both from memory and from other books we had purchased at the conference. Next, someone read *Walking Through a Wall*, a hilarious prose poem by Louis Jenkins, who brilliantly satirizes the absurdities of the modern world, but leaves a thought-provoking inference at the end.

Walking Through a Wall

Unlike flying or astral projection, walking through walls is a totally Earth-related craft, but a bit more interesting than pot making or driftwood lamps. I got started at a picnic up in Bowstring in the northern part of the state. A fellow walked through a brick wall right there in the park. I said, "Say, I want to try that." Stone walls are best, then brick and wood. Wooden walls with fiberglass insulation and steel doors aren't so good. They won't hurt you. If your wall walking is done properly, both you and the wall are left intact. It is just that they aren't pleasant somehow. The worst things are wire fences, maybe it's the molecular structure of the alloy or just the amount of give in a fence, I don't know, but I've torn my jacket and lost my hat in a lot of fences. The best approach to a wall is, first, two hands placed flat against the surface; it's a matter of concentration and just the right pressure. You will feel the dry, cool inner wall with your fingers, then there is a moment of total darkness before you step through on the other side.

LOUIS JENKINS

We continued to laugh and tell jokes until we could stay awake no longer. As I was falling asleep, I realized that I had not laughed that much in at least a decade. I remembered, as I had once told Mickey, the prisoner at DCI who had screamed out his rage at me at the beginning of a workshop, that joy can always be found underneath our sorrow.

Finally, on the fourth day of the conference, I was able to tell Malidoma the whole story of why I had come to see him. He told me without hesitation and with emphasis that, no, my work was not over—that I still had much work to do. I told him of the idea I had of working with ex-offenders on the outside. He said, "That's it. Why don't you go and do that?"

"Because I don't have the money to do it, nor can I find the funding," I said. He then looked at me like I was not seeing the obvious. "You just don't get this, do you? Money is the least of your worries. The money to do your work is already there, and it's been there all along, waiting for you in the spirit world. And you're doing all the right things to get it. You just haven't received it yet. All you have to do is to go back and continue the same things you've been doing, and you'll get all you need." He spoke with such authority that there was no way I could not believe his words. Then he nailed it on the wall for me when he said, "You see, the spirits would never lead you into something and not provide you with the means to do it." At that moment, I actually felt the fear that I had endured for months transform into a simple conviction that I would be okay.

Upon my return to New Orleans, I called Bob Howsen's secretary for the fourth time and asked for a meeting. This time, she got out his schedule and gave me an appointment in early December. Mr. Howsen definitely liked the idea of a re-entry program for recently released prisoners and wanted me to immediately present the idea to the entire Business Council. A week or so later his chief counsel, Fred Baldwin, called to say that the idea would have to be presented first to the Business Council's crime committee, which was chaired by David Hunt, CEO of Consolidated Natural Gas Producing Co. When Fred called about our proposal, Mr. Hunt told him that the committee's "plate was full."

Upon hearing this, I asked Fred, "Would it hurt for me to call him myself?"

"Take your best shot," he said.

So I did. I called and introduced myself to Mr. Hunt's secretary, explaining who I had contacted and what they had said. She calmly listened and told me that Mr. Hunt was busy. So, once again, I left my number. This time, my call was returned in short order by the company's public relations manager, Rodney Ackerman, who listened to my spiel, which by now had begun to sound, to me, like a broken record. It turned out that Rodney lived in the same condominium complex as Rosie and I, only two doors away. He told me he thought that his boss would like the sound of my idea and that he would present it to him. About ten minutes later, David Hunt called me to get the story firsthand. It so happened that I had just put my double boiler on to make a sauce to accompany the dinner I had prepared. Mr. Hunt and

I talked so long that all the water boiled out of the pot and I could hear it crackling as the chrome began to burn off. But this guy was really listening to me and I was not about to put him on hold. It cost me my double boiler, but it was worth it. By the end of the conversation, I had an appointment with Mr. Hunt's crime committee.

The committee was not scheduled to meet again until February, which meant that we would not be able to come before the entire Business Council until March. Since its next meeting was scheduled for the third week of January, David called an emergency meeting of his committee for seven in the morning on January 13, a Monday, so that our request could be added to their docket.

I continued to go into the city with Rosie on occasion to promote my idea to anyone who would listen. Often, I would drop her off at the district attorney's office several hours before a meeting. I used the lobby of a local hospital as a temporary office. By Louisiana law, hospital pay phones required only a dime to place a call, so I kept phone expenses down and had a quiet, comfortable place to work and free parking. One particular day, however, I had several important calls to make and needed privacy to be as effective as possible. I called a lawyer friend, Chris Guidroz, whom I had recently met in a James Hillman study group, and asked if I could come by his office and make a few of these calls. He knew of my struggles to bring this program to life. He answered, "Of course you can. I don't know why I haven't thought of this before. Come on over and I'll get you set up." As it turned out, his firm occupied the entire thirtieth floor of a large office building in the heart of the downtown business district. He and his secretary, Patty, met me in the lobby and took me to one of their spare offices, where she arranged a desk for me with all the amenities of a modern law office. I had my own phone line, access to a copier, a fax machine, voice mail and any assistance I needed. It was an outside office with a magnificent panoramic view of New Orleans. They told me to consider it their contribution to my efforts until I got the program up and running. I had my own office.

The first phone call I made was to the assistant warden at the Police Barracks. I asked if he would pass a note to Malcolm to call so I could give him some good news. I also wanted to encourage him that, as things were going, I believed that good news about his pardon also would be forthcoming. He was, of course, happy about the encouraging developments and was awestruck by their synchronicity with Malidoma's foresight. Nevertheless, as I listened I heard much more despair in his voice than before. Although my hope for the future was mounting, I now knew in my heart and in my dreams what it meant to have a loved one in prison, to lay awake at night and worry about that person's safety and well-being. The experience resonated deep in my bones. Our society has very little empathy for the families of prisoners who know that, every hour of the day and night, their child, spouse or sibling is vulnerable to nightmarish danger.

A day or so after New Year's Day I made an appointment to visit again with some members of the pardon board with whom I had previously spoken about getting the governor to sign Malcolm's pardon. At our previous meetings, I developed the impression that they had learned to listen to pleas such as mine while on automatic pilot. In desperation, I tried one last explanation of who Malcolm Hill was. I told them, "If I were dying and there was no one in my family who could finish raising my sons, and I could ask Malcolm to take them, I could die in peace."

"Oh, I see," said Nettie Millican. This time, I got the impression that she really heard me. Perhaps what touched her was that, as a black woman who had served on the pardon board for seven years, she had never heard a white man say something so profound about a prisoner. She told me sincerely that she would like to help, but that, in reality, I had only one hope—I would have to convince a powerful member of the state legislature, someone "very close" to the governor, to petition for Malcolm's pardon. I reasoned that since our governor was considered by many to be the most corrupt in the country, I must find the legislator I believed was the most corrupt in the state.

That afternoon, I called the person who seemed to fit that profile. I explained to him that Malcolm was a model prisoner and an integral part of an ongoing university research project to rehabilitate prisoners. I then explained to him that the pardon board had recommended that I find the most powerful legislator in the state. I told him, "To me, that means you, senator."

"Well, I think there is probably something I can do to help," he answered.

The next day I received the most despondent letter yet from Malcolm. I immediately wrote him back, "Hang in there, Malcolm. Freedom is just around the corner." Two days later, the senator's secretary called me from Baton Rouge to relay a message from Governor Edwards' chief counsel's office, a letter that stated that the governor had agreed to sign Malcolm's pardon. I dared not call Malcolm and tell him without proof, and the only proof would be to see the pardon myself. The next morning about eleven, the phone rang and I heard Malcolm's voice shouting, "Bob, I'm goin' home! The governor signed my pardon this morning and my mother is on her way to pick me up now! I was working in the kitchen and the supervisor came up to me and said, 'Malcolm, the governor just signed your pardon. You're a free man as of right now. I'll get you a ride back to the barracks to get your stuff, or you can just walk out the door.'" Then Malcolm said that his mother had just stepped out of her car outside in the parking lot and that he had to go.

I wished with all my heart that I could have been there to see him "step off the curb" and take his first steps as a free man in more than twelve years, but I knew that those moments and the next few days belonged to him and his family. During that time I called to tell him that I hoped he could accompany me and attend the meeting with the Business Council crime committee. He agreed and told me that he was very anxious to see Perry, though he did not explain why. We arranged for him to catch a bus into New Orleans and spend the weekend with Perry. I was to come into town on Sunday, have lunch with the two of them and then bring Malcolm home with me.

Perry, who had been home for a year, lived in the Magnolia Project, one of many federal housing projects in New Orleans infested with crime and violence. There, Perry was well known as someone not to mess with. He and members of his family had controlled the drug trafficking in the area for some time. Since Perry was no longer in the business and, therefore, not in any competition for territory, he was no longer considered a threat.

The plan worked fine. I picked them up on Washington Street, not far from Perry's apartment. We made quite a spectacle of ourselves shouting and hugging each other right out there in front of God and all of Perry's neighbors. We bought burgers and headed for Audubon Park, where we found a quiet table to eat and reminisce. During lunch, my mind kept looking back down the road that had led us to this joyful and unpredictable gathering. Reflecting on my own journey, I wondered, *Who is this person sitting in my body feeling overjoyed at having a burger in Audubon Park with two black men recently released from prison for drug dealing and bank robbery, together celebrating the miracle of our freedom and our transformations into this brotherhood?*

During lunch, Perry told us the story of how close he had come to going right back to prison. He had struggled since his release to keep a job, which was essential because it was a condition of his parole. But his first employer, who was aware of this requirement, took full advantage of Perry's situation, working him sixty hours a week in his auto body shop and paying him $120 a week. He had threatened to call Perry's parole officer, Janet Rivard, if he walked off the job. Fortunately for Perry, though, Janet was willing to let him quit the job in order to look for another.

A series of jobs followed, including one cleaning out chemical tanks for Exxon. This multibillion dollar oil company hired part-timers for such duties so they would not have to pay medical benefits if the chemicals made them ill somewhere down the line. When the job was completed, Perry was laid off. Other jobs had also ended with cutbacks and layoffs, often leaving him discouraged. One day, when he handed his son, Bébé, a few dollars for something at school, the boy asked his father, "Where did you get that money, from Mama?" The question shot straight through Perry's heart, which was already filled with shame over his numerous failures as a man and a father. It would be so easy, he knew, to buy a small quantity of cocaine, cook it up into rocks and sell them on the street, where he could make $1,000 in an afternoon. He had been very successful during his days as a drug dealer until he was stopped for a traffic violation and was caught with a trunk full of drugs.

"'One time I was thinkin',' " he said, "just one hit to get some money in my pocket while I search for the next job." This last wound to his manhood delivered so innocently by his son had sent him temporarily over the line as he made plans for one last sojourn into the world of a drug dealer. Tucking the bag of rocks under his belt buckle, he headed out to one of his old familiar street corners to make his scores. No sooner had he arrived than two police cruisers came screaming up on a bust of some other suspected dealers. Immediately, they braced Perry against one of the cars and began patting him down. The cop put his hand directly over the bag and, by some miracle, missed it. The whole time this was going on, Perry said, he was not thinking of his wife or even his son. All he could think of was how sad I would be when I heard that he had been busted for intent to distribute. He went home, flushed the rocks down the toilet and vowed never again— and this time he meant for good.

After lunch and hours of celebration, as Malcolm and I were headed across Lake Pontchartrain for his first visit to my home, Malcolm explained his reason for wanting to first spend some time with Perry. He said that he had not been able to sleep at home for the four nights he was there. As well as he could, he explained the discomfort of not being around anyone who understood what he was talking about when he described his prison experience. The Friday and Saturday nights at Perry's apartment had been his first two nights of sleep since being home.

When we arrived at my house, we discovered that Rosie had sprinkled red rose petals on the walkway and front steps and had hung balloons and put up a large sign above the door, "Welcome." For dessert, she fulfilled a request Malcolm made long ago for strawberry shortcake, serving it up with a brightly burning sparkler in the middle. After dinner, Malcolm told us that we had finally answered the one last burning question in his heart about us. He still had not been sure that, once he was released, "You would really welcome me into your home in your white neighborhood." He had always felt that it was one thing to be his friend in prison, but another thing for Rosie and I to bring him into our home and introduce him to family and neighbors. Malcolm explained that his experiences had always taught him to fear and dislike white people, but that Rosie and I had changed all of that for him. Yet another extraordinary transition had taken place.

It was Sunday, January 12. The next morning we would meet with the Business Council crime committee. Malcolm told us that he was wearing all the clothes he owned. He thought that his mother would have at least enough money to buy him a pair of jeans and a shirt, but that wasn't the case. After twelve years in prison, the only clothing awaiting him at home was a pair of shoes his mother had saved. He had the shoes restained and polished. I dressed him in a white shirt and beige pants I borrowed from a friend, my old blue blazer, a pair of my socks and one of my ties, which I knotted for him.

After breakfast, we went down to the car for the twenty-mile drive to the city, where we would meet with David Hunt's committee. The sun was still aglow on the dawn horizon. As we closed the car doors, through the windshield we saw the dark silhouette of a hawk gliding only a few feet away, ever so smoothly across our path in front of the car. Never once did it flap its wings. Malcolm and I looked at each other smiling. Surely, it was a good sign and seemed to be no accident.

The boardroom of Consolidated Natural Gas was as richly furnished and luxurious as I had imagined it would be. The solid-wood conference table was surrounded by plush arm-chairs that rocked back to a very comfortable position, one that I was careful not to assume. Mike Sport had told me that the largest sum of money the council had given out to any program was $35,000. We had decided not to risk being obvious that we knew this and ask for only $30,000. I was praying for $25,000.

The meeting began with pleasantries and introductions. Mr. Hunt did not look anything like I had imagined him. I'd thought he would look like a yuppie, but instead, he was dressed in a dark suit, wore rather thick glasses on his round face and had a distinguished head of gray hair.

I began the meeting by introducing myself and Malcolm, careful to leave out anything about Malcolm's background. I knew that he would tell them in his own good time. I nervously glanced at my pages of notes and stammered through the basics of our proposal. I knew I did not have to call on Malcolm to speak, for I had spent enough hours in group sessions with him to know that in time he would feel moved to do so. When he did, it would come straight from the heart and would begin with, "My name's Malcolm." I had come to the final descriptions of the proposed program that detailed our plan to arrange job placements for program graduates.

At this point, Dan Drieling, the senior vice president of Freeport-McMoRan, a *Fortune 500* company, spoke up. Seated opposite me at the conference table, he was a very distinguished looking executive. He had been recruited from the FBI to head up corporate security for his company. During subsequent meetings, I became aware of his remarkable intelligence and capacity to find the weaknesses in a person's arguments and to confront them about loopholes. Mr. Dreiling asked, "Where are you going to find all these jobs? There are no jobs out there! You're going to have to get these people to be patient. How are you going to do that?"

There was total quiet as I sat, choking silently, with nothing to say. Then to my immediate right I heard, "My name's Malcolm." I didn't look over at him, but I could feel his intensity. He told the committee of his release only eight days before from twelve years of prison for bank robbery. He told them whose clothes he was wearing. I wondered if anyone on this committee had ever been in the same room with a bank robber or anyone else who had been to prison. All their eyes were fixed on Malcolm, and, if you would have silenced his voice, you could have heard a pin drop.

Looking across the table at Dan Dreiling, Malcolm said, "It would be one thing for you to drive up here in your Mercedes"—I thought I was going to die—"and tell these people that they will have to be patient. But it would be entirely different for me to sit down with them while I am going through the same crisis as they are and say to them, 'We have to help each other make it through this and not get impatient.'" As I looked around at the committee, it seemed the embodiment of a frozen moment in time, so I was not sure how Mr. Dreiling or anyone else had taken his words.

After a few more exchanges, we were invited to wait outside the conference room while the committee conducted a
closed-door discussion and a vote. When we returned, Mr.
Hunt announced to us that the committee had voted to recommend to the Business Council that they provide us with a
challenge grant of $150,000 over the next year and a half.
This meant that we would have to raise a matching amount
over that period of time in order to receive the funds. He then
said that each member of the council would be asked to individually contribute to the matching funds. I thought about
the hawk as I listened to David's words.

David Hunt then asked if there was any further business.
Malcolm said, "Yes. I need a job now. If anyone knows of a job
that I could get until we get this program up and running, I
would take it."

Dan Dreiling asked, "What kind of job do you want?"
Malcolm responded that he would do anything, but that he
had heard of a job at the Hilton Hotel and had put in an
application for it on Saturday. Several business cards came
sliding across the table. But Dreiling interrupted, saying, "I've
got this one, gentlemen."

As the meeting adjourned, we stood up and began shaking
hands with those standing around us while we thanked them.
I noticed Dan Dreiling coming around the table toward
Malcolm. He smiled warmly as he offered a handshake and
said, "Well, Malcolm, I think you're gonna need a better

haberdasher than Bob." That afternoon, Mr. Dreiling called Paul Buckley, general manager of the downtown Hilton Hotel, where Malcolm had put in his application. According to the story that he would later tell us, Mr. Buckley willingly agreed to give Malcolm the job. He himself had grown up in a tough neighborhood in South Boston and was familiar with the troubled life. He told Dreiling that it would make no difference to him what charge had sent Malcolm to prison, but he was curious. Dreiling answered, "I'm not sure, but I think it was for killing a hotel manager."

That afternoon, Mr. Buckley phoned the number Malcolm had on his application and left the message that he wanted to meet anyone whom Dan Dreiling would recommend. He invited Malcolm to come to his office at nine the next morning. When Malcolm arrived, Buckley offered coffee and refreshments before giving him a tour of the hotel and then hiring him for the open position.

I told the Business Council members that I would consider affiliating the program with a university, despite my experience with LSU. The connection that LSU and DCI held with the state government had turned out to be unhealthful for cutting-edge endeavors like ours. The experience had left me somewhat shell-shocked with regards to the academic world at large, but especially toward state universities.

In a subsequent conversation, Herschel Abbott, CEO of Bell South of Louisiana and one of the Business Council members, asked me if I had considered affiliating the project with Tulane University. I told him that during earlier, informal conversations with the heads of psychiatry and social work at Tulane, I had not sensed the kind of enthusiasm from them that would generate the kind of support this work required. He suggested I have a visit with the dean of public health and added, "By the way, I'm chairman of the board of governors of Tulane Medical Center. Let me know if they aren't interested in this program."

Within the hour I called the dean for an appointment and discovered that Herschel had already made the introductory contact for me and set up the meeting for the next day. The dean, Harrison Spencer, M.D., was a tall man in his mid-fifties with thinning hair and a friendly but serious look in his eye. Also present was the department head of Community Health Sciences, Elizabeth Bennett, who had a Ph.D. in nursing. A pleasant looking woman in her sixties, she seemed content to sit back and listen to the discussion unfold. Dean Spencer told me of his thoughts on the study of violence as a public health issue. The idea that violence could be preventable, according to him, made it a public health issue.

I might have finally come to the right place, I thought. I began to explain to them the concepts of community building, noting that they are based on the principle of extraordinary respect for every human being, in spite of what was done in his or her past. As I went on, I noticed that Betty had her eyes closed and was nodding in complete agreement with me. At that moment, I knew I had found a home for the project. The process of our affiliation with Tulane, including my faculty appointment as clinical assistant professor, began that very day. Besides its prominent standing in the academic world, Tulane's appeal was that it was a private university and therefore not under state control.

Within weeks, I was able to write a grant to the local office of the Job Training Partnership Act (JTPA) and get the matching funds the Business Council had offered. Within the next year and a half, their contributions and matching funds would reach over $750,000. In addition, the JTPA grant included the payment of a small hourly training wage for the participants and the installation of a computer-learning lab, complete with adult-education software. The stipend amounted to only $2.50 per hour, but at least it would be something participants could use for transportation and lunch.

The grant also provided a salary and training for the computer lab instructor, so I began a search for someone to fill that position. Since we were going to ask local businesses to hire former offenders who graduated from the program, I knew that we would have to set the example. I immediately thought of Perry Bernard. Though I knew he had no experience with computers, I also knew that he was keenly intelligent. What an example he could set for all employers, and what a role model he would be for all our participants.

Together, he and I entered the weeklong training sponsored by IBM, the company that had built the lab. After only three days, I could see that Perry had the procedures well in hand, so I withdrew from the school to answer one last challenge to my commitment and to this calling.

I had received a call from Dr. John Allen, my friend at LSU Medical School in Shreveport, the man who had wanted me to take over the dean of student affairs job he was leaving. The faculty member who had stepped into that position had suffered a massive stroke and died instantly. According to Dr. Allen, the job was mine to accept or turn down. In my heart and soul, I knew that I could not walk away from what we had already created in New Orleans, but I decided to interview for the job anyway. To those around me, it was a shock that I would even consider this interview. Perhaps I wanted to test my own commitment and perhaps I felt I owed it to my two sons who still lived in Shreveport to give the job my complete consideration. This would most likely be the last realistic opportunity I would ever have to return home and live near them. If I was going to turn this job down, though, as I felt certain I would, I wanted a complete understanding of just what I was walking away from.

With my friend Dr. Allen as chairperson, my interview before the search committee went as I expected. My next meeting was with Dr. Ike Muslow, the chancellor of the medical center. I had known him indirectly for years, having attended school with his daughter since junior high. I once saw him as a patient for back pain after I was discharged from the Army. I had always felt honored and respected him for the simple fact that he always remembered my name and asked how my back was doing, how my practice was going and so on. He was Jewish, and I had often thought that if *I* were Jewish, I would want this man for my Rabbi.

Our conversation on this day was inspiring to me, as always. I brought him up to date on the changes I had made in my life. When I told him of the most recent developments with the project in New Orleans, he said, "You know, that work sounds a lot more important than this job." I agreed, knowing it meant that I was turning down an exceptional offer. I thanked "my rabbi" and left with this answer. My home was no longer in Shreveport, Louisiana.

After three years of learning and soul-searching, of laughter and loss, of struggling with unemployment and the pardon board and seeing a few miracles along the way, Malcolm and I, and now Perry, finally discovered a path we could all walk together. We found the gift we could offer our village—a way of fighting crime and violence without doing further harm.

The Guest House

This being human is a guest house.
Every morning a new arrival.

A joy, a depression, a meanness,
Some momentary awareness comes
As an unexpected visitor.

Welcome and entertain them all!
Even if they're a crowd of sorrows,
Who violently sweep your house
Empty of its furniture,
Still, treat each guest honorably.
He may be clearing you out
For some new delight

The dark thought, the shame, the malice,
Meet them at the door laughing,
And invite them in.

Be grateful for whoever comes,
Because each has been sent
As a guide from beyond.

Rumi
(translated by Coleman Barks)

7

Grace, Healing and Forgiveness

*I*n November 1993, Project Return opened its doors for the first time. We began with a staff of four. Malcolm and I planned to conduct the community-building workshops and classes on basic literacy, employability and life skills, while Perry ran the computer lab for the more advanced learners. Cecile Scorza, who had recently retired from twenty-two years as an executive secretary for Shell Oil Company, became our secretary.

I anticipated that I would encounter difficulty in leasing office space, and I was not disappointed. We limited our search to the downtown area since all of the public bus lines terminated there, but we could not find a building that would lease to us. When I finally discovered the building I wanted, only to be turned down again, I refused to take no for an answer. I appealed to the leasing agent to allow me to meet with the building owner. Only a few minutes into that meeting, he abruptly interrupted me. "I'm not going to lease you this space for the money," he said, "I'm going to do it because I like what you're trying to do with this program." I was completely surprised by the bizarre timing of his statement. It was as out of context as the Business Council's grant of $150,000 when we had only asked for $30,000. I thanked him sincerely, reflecting once again on Malidoma's assertion that the spirits do not lead us into something without providing us with the means to do it.[†]

---

† UNTIL ONE IS COMMITTED
Until one is committed, there is hesitancy, the chance to draw back, always ineffectiveness. Concerning all acts of initiative (and creation) there is one elementary truth, the ignorance of which kills countless ideas and splendid plans: that the moment one definitely commits oneself, then Providence moves too. All sorts of things occur to help one that would never otherwise have occurred. A whole stream of events issues from the decision, raising in one's favor all manner of unforeseen incidents and meetings and material assistance, which no man could have dreamed would have come his way.

> Whatever you can do,
> or dream you can, begin it.
> Boldness has genius,
> power and magic in it.
> > Goethe (translated by Robert Bly)

> Move from within,
> Don't move the way fear wants you to.
>
> Begin a foolish project.
> Noah did!
>
> Begin your life's dream.
> Remember the promise you made before you came here.
> > Rumi (translated by Coleman Barks)

Malcolm and Perry had put the word out on the streets that we were opening our doors, and together we had solicited for applicants at parole offices and addiction treatment centers around the city. On the first day of our program, twenty-nine people showed up. All were men, and all black, except one. They had served anywhere from one to five terms in prison on convictions ranging from drug dealing to armed robbery and murder. Our only plan was to build community once we had enrolled about fifty members. But until then, we would have to think of something to do with these men.

After interviewing these twenty-nine men to discover who they were and why they were there, Malcolm asked me, "What now?" I suggested that we form a circle and see what would happen.

A minute after the introductions, Gerald Walker, the only white man present, broke the ice for us. Gerald had come to us from one of the homeless shelters in the city. Sixty-four years old and toothless, he wore an old western straw hat and the blue-jean jacket and pants he had worn home from prison. His voice began to choke with emotion as he said simply, "All my life, I've wanted to sit in a circle like this and just talk." That moment was the perfect introduction to Project Return.

More remarkable moments were to follow. During the community-building workshop that followed, a fellow prison-mate of Malcolm's, Billy Jacobs, said that during his twenty-one years at Angola, he had to sleep with one hand covering his throat, a large book on his chest under his clothing and a knife taped to his other hand—the same conditions Malcolm had described to me three years earlier. These were standard precautions if a man was to remain alive through the night. Billy's worst experience, however, involved being stuck in the dormitory with a new prisoner he described as completely crazy and who kept setting people on fire while they slept. Even though this man set fire to seven people, killing two of them, the correctional officers would not remove him from the general population. Finally, after no one in the dormitory had been able to sleep for three straight months, they decided that someone had to kill this sad, crazy man.

The man who killed him had come along with Billy to Project Return and was sitting next to me in the workshop. With deep sorrow in his voice, he told everyone, "We really didn't hate this guy. He was just crazy and we were all goin' crazy around him. I did it quick, so he didn't suffer."

I leaned over to Malcolm, who was sitting to my right, and whispered, "I thought you already told me the worst stories." I thought I had heard it all in the three years of community building in the prison system, but now we were working with people who brought even more of the horrors of prison and stories they could not tell anyone at home. I got the impression that my learning curve had only begun to climb.

One thing that made my level of understanding soar was learning about the depths of poverty in which our participants were living. Despite all I had discovered at DCI about the world inside and outside our prison walls, I was not aware that such poverty existed in the United States. This lesson was driven home one day when a participant brought his three-year-old stepdaughter to the program because there was no one to watch her at home. During the lunch hour, Malcolm overheard him ask another participant who had brought a sandwich if he would share a piece of bread with the little girl. The sacrifices this man was making to turn his life around became clear to me when Malcolm told me that he was a former drug dealer who could have left at that moment and made $1,000 by the end of day in his old profession.

On occasion, one of us would run into an old acquaintance from DCI on the streets and invite him to come by and sign up for the next class, or just come by and visit. Most were struggling with their old addictions, with family problems or with offers from former partners in the drug business who were always offering them crack to sell. Their families, for the most part, were either "on their ass all the time" or on crack all the time.

Leon Courtney, who had been in the Dorm 7 group at DCI, had been a highly successful drug dealer before his arrest. Now he had a job baking pizza dough for $6 an hour on the night shift of a French Quarter restaurant. Since his release on parole, he had managed to stay straight for the first few months but was plagued by nightmares of going back to prison. On the day he heard that our program had opened, he came rushing into our office like a man on the edge of coming completely apart.

Leon had been trying for the last few months to renew his driver's license so that, instead of relying on his wife, he could drive himself to his job. She had to get up at four in the morning to pick him up before she went to work at eight because he could not drive. The department of motor vehicles refused to grant him a new license until he paid off a $200 fine for failing to renew the tag on his car while he was in prison. He also owed another $380 in fines for two traffic tickets, one of which was issued seven years ago, before his arrest. The second ticket was issued in Leon's name *while he was serving time in prison.* He was afraid to risk an argument with the bureau clerk because she was in a state police uniform and could, with one phone call to his parole officer, have him arrested and sent back to prison for another six years.

Leon had become even more worried recently. While having lunch with his wife, his ex-drug partner walked up to them and dropped the keys to a new Jaguar onto the table, saying, "That's yours." This was, of course, an invitation for Leon to rejoin his old partner in the drug business, where the two had previously made $50,000 per week. Though Leon returned the keys, he must have had second thoughts about the $6 per hour he earned at the pizza restaurant. Then, to top it off, the week before his visit to Project Return, while he was out for a walk near his house, two policemen had pulled over and signaled him to stop. They called Leon by his old street name, Mr. Lucky, and told him they had heard he was back in town and just wanted to let him know that now this was "their neighborhood." They each handed Leon a business card and told him to call when he was ready to go back to work again. If Leon went back into the drug business, they expected to get their cut of his profit.

After all of these events, Leon had become so severely paranoid that he was scared to leave his house. He told me that he felt as if he were back in prison. In spite of the sadness of his story, I couldn't help being aware that, compared to most of the stories I had heard, Leon really was one of the lucky ones. He owned his home, which was a duplex, and rented half of it. He had a car, a skill, a job and a wife who loved him. What he said he needed most, however, was some-one to talk to, someone who could understand how he felt and what he'd been through.

————

Others from the DCI program were not so lucky. A few weeks before Christmas, I was on my way back to the office after meeting Rosie for lunch at the faculty club. I felt con-tent to be working again, and very blessed to finally have this dream program up and running.

As I waited to cross at the traffic light, I glanced behind me and noticed a tall man who stood leaning against the bank building. I immediately assumed he was drunk, since, except for an occasional twitch, he seemed almost asleep. He held the familiar brown bag in his right hand, stuck in the pocket of his olive, drab Army overcoat. He had a full head of white hair, a mustache and a goatee that contrasted with his midnight dark skin. His face looked familiar and, for a moment, I thought I recognized him. Then I glanced down at his feet and I was certain. I stepped in front of him, looked up at his face, which was about seven inches higher than mine and said, "Excuse me, are you Joe Stanley?" Joe was the man who had read the Rudyard Kipling poem "If" to the young men in the first workshop at DCI with Dorm 7.

His red swollen eyes slowly began to open. When they met mine they suddenly opened a bit wider. I knew he recognized me, but he lowered his head again and closed his eyes as he faintly answered, "No."

I was ready to leave him alone if that was what he wanted, but I said in parting, "Well, you remind me of a dear friend I used to have named Joe Stanley." I paused for just a second more. Without looking at me, he said, "It's me, Bob. How did you find me? How'd you remember my name, my whole name?"

"Joe," I said, "I could never forget you, your name or your big feet."

Joe reached down and grabbed me and held me and wept openly, saying that he did not want me to ever see him like this. "How is your sweet wife, Rosemary? She was always so kind to me, Bob. I don't want her to see me like this, please don't tell her you saw me." He kept on weeping. I noticed that the people walking by looked frightened and confused at the scene. Joe went on, mostly repeating himself about Rosemary, begging me not to tell her I'd seen him.

He then said he needed to make a phone call. I invited him up to Project Return to use my phone and so he could see what we were doing up there. Taking him by the arm, I escorted him across the street to our building, where Perry was taking a break out front on a bench. He recognized Joe and knew immediately what I was doing. As Perry approached us, I was struck by the contrast between the two, a contrast that was not apparent when I'd first met the two men in prison. There, they'd worn the same blue jeans and light-blue shirt with "DCI" painted in bright, reflective six-inch letters, front and back, top and bottom. They'd had the same prisoner demeanor about them, at times quiet, at other times angry, depressed, defiant.

The difference between them now was dramatic. Perry looked healthy and sharp, with clothes that fit well and were starched and ironed. Joe could see the difference and told Perry how great it was to see him doing so well.

As we walked down the hall toward my office, Joe began to

weep again, saying to me, "Bob, you just gotta let me go. I'm no good, Bob. I'm a con man. I've always been a con man an' I always will be."

"That's all right, Joe, just come on in and use my phone and we'll talk a little and you can go take care of your business, okay?"

"Bob, please, don't let Rosemary see me like this," he continued to plead.

"She doesn't work here, Joe. She's at the district attorney's office over on Tulane and Broad."

"Please don't tell her you saw me, Bob. Please!"

We finally reached my office, where someone got him a cup of coffee and we began to talk. Joe continued to insist, "Bob, you just gotta let me go, 'cause I'm just an ole con man."

"So am I, Joe," I said. "That's probably one of the reasons I've always liked you so much, 'cause we have that in common. See, I conned people into letting me do this, made them think I knew what I was talking about. The Business Council, the university, even the U.S. Department of Justice. They've given me a total of a half-million dollars so far." His eyes were opening a little more now in surprise at what I was saying. "Everybody's got a con, Joe—doctors, preachers, lawyers. Some of us, like you and me, have better ones than others. The only difference is when we use it, and for what."

I called Malcolm on the intercom. He and Joe greeted each other as he entered my office, and the contrast between the two was as striking as before with Perry. Together, Malcolm and I invited Joe to come in off the streets one last time. Joe responded that at present he was living in Mississippi, but he would think about us. I "loaned" him $20 and he was gone.

Neither Malcolm nor I expected to see him again. However, about three weeks later, while on my way to teach my class at Tulane, I saw Joe walking down the street. He was wearing the same drab, olive-colored overcoat, but he was walking straight and looked clean. He smiled this time when he recognized me and we hugged. I immediately noticed that his eyes were clear and opened wide and that he was sober and probably had been for a couple of weeks or so. I told him I was in a hurry to teach a class. As we parted, he said he would be up to see us soon. I remain hopeful for him.

During the Christmas holidays, Malcolm and Perry warned me to expect an increase in drug relapse among our class members. Of course that would be likely, I thought. For them and for so many others, the holidays are the season of despair and loneliness, when all failures are reproclaimed and unhealed wounds reopen and rankle with shame. We suggested to the men that if they could just keep their lines of communication open with each other, this could become a time when their community building would offer its greatest advantage. The plan worked well. Though some men relapsed anyway, and a few were thrown in jail by their parole officers, most reported finding the requisite support from each other.

In the end, they expressed gratitude that they had been able to keep their freedom.

—————

On Monday morning, January 10, 1994, only months after the program began, I met face-to-face with my greatest crisis yet: I became dizzy while getting ready to leave for the office. Feeling like I might pass out, I called to Rosie and tried to make it down the stairs. On the way, the dizziness blurred into unconsciousness and a seizure as I tumbled onto the kitchen floor.

My next memory was sitting up on the couch and realizing there were two paramedics and a policeman standing in the doorway. They asked me to lie down on a stretcher so they could take me to the hospital. As I did, I was unable to breathe and began gasping for air. The paramedic placed an oxygen cup over my face, which at first panicked me with claustrophobia, but I regained enough reasoning ability to know that the pure oxygen would help me.

The next few hours were mostly lost in a blur of sirens, the inside of the emergency room and CT scans at the local hospital in Slidell. Sometime after Rosie joined me in the emergency room, I had a second seizure, although I do not remember it. My next memory was of an East Indian radiologist who walked into the room and was holding up one of my X rays. He pointed to a tumor the size of a golf ball that was on the left side of my brain and offered a probable diagnosis of metastatic melanoma. The prognosis for recovery from such a tumor is practically nonexistent, and the survival rate is about four months.

My first reaction, which flashed through my mind for only a split second, was one of elation—as if I were a prisoner who had just been told that he could go home. I briefly imagined my dying as an ecstatic journey with the kind of anticipation I used to feel when planning a cross-country flight alone in my small plane. My second reaction was a feeling of terrible grief when I saw the tears in Rosie's eyes, and I realized that I would be leaving her and my sons behind. My third, however, was to remember Malidoma's words that my work was not finished. I was immediately certain this was still true. I wondered at that moment if the spirits could be calling me to continue this work on the other side, in the spirit world. If that was their call, I felt I could accept my death. Furthermore, I felt that if the spirits had blessed this journey, then Rosie and my sons would be all right. Somehow, I felt strongly that Malidoma was correct, that either my dying must be for a good purpose or I was not going to die. For that reason, fear never entered the room. Instead, a sense of grace remained with me during the week that followed, in spite of the sorrow. The only dread I felt was of the suffering that lie ahead from dying from brain cancer. I resolved, however, that there would be none of the traditional remedies such as chemotherapy or radiation therapy. If the spirits had called me to move on, I was ready.

The physician in charge recommended that I be transported to Tulane Hospital, where my insurance benefits would save us a considerable sum of money. We were told that we were facing at least $350,000 in expenses. Before leaving the hospital by ambulance, I asked Rosie to call Malidoma; Martín Prechtel, a Mayan Shaman; and John Witherspoon, a young Ojibwa shaman. The latter two I had met through Malidoma at another Men's Conference in Minnesota a few months before. I did not necessarily want them to try to save me with their prayers and magic, but whatever journey lay ahead for me, I wanted them to know about it.

Malcolm met us at the Tulane emergency room, before I was taken to intensive care. He was devastated and told me that he wondered at first how he was going to carry on the program without me and my professional credentials. In spite of this, he shared my conviction that our work would somehow continue. Rosie asked him if he would mind calling the three healers for her while she made the necessary calls to my family and hers. He was immediately able to get in touch with everyone but Martín, who was in the southern part of Arizona and far from a telephone. All Malcolm could get was the number of a pay phone at a ranch house an hour's drive from where Martín was gathering that season's herbs and doing ceremony in the desert with his son, Santiago. Malcolm called that number, but, in his desperate confusion, he asked the person who answered for Malidoma instead of Martín. By a serendipitous touch of fate, Martín just happened to be standing next to the pay phone and responded when he recognized Malidoma's name. Martín immediately agreed to help, and he and his son spent the next seventeen hours in the desert doing a healing ceremony for me. Malidoma, John and other friends began prayers and ceremonies also.

The next day, when Malcolm came to see me, the room was filled with members of my family who had driven down that morning. He came straight over to the bed and placed his arms around me in an embrace. We both wept. Then he turned to my mother and stepfather and said, "I would like to show you where Bob works and what he has been doing."

It had always been a source of great sadness to me that my family, including my four sons—Bobby, twenty-four; Jeff, twenty-three; Adam, nineteen; Joel, thirteen—had never understood why I had given up my successful career as a dentist to do something as "crazy" as working with prisoners and former offenders. My sons were especially confused because their grandfather—my stepfather and the family patriarch—withheld his blessing from me. They knew on some level that I was doing something worthy of a deep commitment, but they also loved and respected their grandfather and his values. Holly, as he is known, was a highly successful business executive who had retired a few years earlier from the position of senior vice president of Pennzoil.

As Malcolm showed my family around the Project Return offices, he saw the light of understanding and then pride slowly dawn in their faces. My mother turned to Malcolm as they were about to leave, and said, "No matter what happens, you *must* carry on this work." When they returned to the hospital room my stepfather said, in front of the entire family, "I am ashamed of the way I have treated you, Bob. I didn't really understand what you were doing." So far, I had lived without his blessing and could have carried on further without it. But receiving it in front of my sons meant everything to me, since that meant they would no longer have to live with confusion about their father and the path he had chosen.

—◆—

During the week that followed, I went through a barrage of diagnostic procedures aimed at confirming the seriousness and the exact source of my condition. Since the tumor was considered metastatic, it had to have come from somewhere else in the body. By Thursday, my physician, a neurosurgeon, felt certain that the diagnosis was correct, but he thought that the tumor might be operable and offered to conduct exploratory surgery the next day to find out. Rosie and my family, including all my sons, asked me to try this approach, so I agreed.

Because the surgery carried a high risk factor, my lawyer

friend, Chris Guidroz, who had provided me with the office at his law firm, drew up my "final papers" and brought them by for me to sign. It was time to say my farewells, just in case. One or two at a time for the next several hours, my sons, my sister, my brother, my parents, my mother-in-law, even my ex-wife, came in and allowed old wounds to heal, leaving me amazed and joyful that I was so loved. Finally, Rosie and I were left alone. Quietly weeping, she climbed into bed with me and we lay there in silence, possibly for the last time.

At the same time that evening, John Witherspoon, the young Ojibwa shaman, was performing a divination ceremony in Minnesota. During that ceremony, he sang and offered gifts of food, tobacco and the scent of burning sweetgrass to the spirits so they would draw near and listen to his prayer. He asked five of his ancestral spirits, three men and two women, to come down and protect me. John was a young medicine man and did not yet have all of his powers, nor had he ever attempted a healing from such a distance. Nonetheless, he told me later that during the ceremony he had seen that the two women had made the journey. He could see them in my hospital room, one of them standing behind me holding my head and the other in front touching my face. Afterward, he called Malcolm and told him he thought I was going to be all right.

That night, Malcolm had a dream that he was riding in the back of a pickup truck with several other people and a small boy wearing a green jacket just like mine, except that this one had a hood that was pulled over the boy's head. Malcolm thought the little boy was me, but he could not see the face under the hood. Suddenly, the truck swerved. The little boy was falling over the side, but Malcolm grabbed him and pulled him back in. When he awoke, he was certain that the dream meant I was going to be all right. He rushed to the hospital to tell me, but I had gone into surgery about 5:30 that morning.

I had asked Rosie to bring me a small rock I had brought home from the lake in Minnesota where I had last made ceremony with the three medicine men. I held the rock in my hand as I was taken into surgery, figuring the nurses would remove it once I was asleep. The surgeon shaved my head and exposed my left temporal bone, underneath which lay the tumor. When he opened up my temporal bone to see if the lesion was operable, he found no tumor at all, only a bit of blood tissue in the place where the tumor had been. Although the neurosurgeon immediately changed his diagnosis to cavernous hemangioma, a tumor of blood tissue, he was honest enough to admit his confusion. "This one fooled me," he said. But I also found out that, on the day before surgery, he and his assistant had told my intensive-care nurse that their tests had confirmed the diagnosis of cancer.

The first thing I remember after surgery was Rosie standing by my bed, holding my hand, saying that I was okay and that we had many more years to be together. The second thing I remember was becoming aware that my sister,

Bettye, had taped the small rock to my hand. Three days later, I left the hospital with a really sore head, looking like a freak with half my hair shaved and metal staples holding my scalp closed. I felt incredibly grateful to my allies who had prayed for me and to my family who had gathered around me when I needed them. Malcolm told me about his dream and about his confusion that the boy's green jacket had a hood. I told him that my jacket had a concealed hood that zipped into the collar.

When I regained some of my strength, I called some of the people who had sung prayers and made ceremony for me. When I reached Martín, he said that I had done all the work and that I was *his* hero. The only sense I could make of his words was that my willingness to accept whatever the spirits had in mind for me was connected to my healing. Perhaps that meant that instead of fighting the cancer, I had embraced it as a catalyst towards my soul's intended journey. Martín explained to me that the body is the world and that the illness in my body was only a metaphor for the disharmony in my outer life. Just as my inner organs needed to come together in community for me to get better, all of the people in my life— Malcolm, my children, my ex-wife, my parents and my other family members—needed to come together in community and mutual understanding of my journey for me to heal.

John Witherspoon returned my call to tell me that the ceremony he performed required a closing, and that I had to be there. Knowing there was no way I could travel to him, he said that as soon as I was well enough, he would drive down from Minnesota to make the closing. He arrived a week later and performed the ceremony with Rosie and me in the upstairs loft of our home. It was a ritual of gratitude to the Great Spirit, our ancestors and our spirit guides—animal, human and otherwise. I offered gifts of tobacco, jade, food and words to all our allies in the invisible world. Remembering a prayer Malidoma taught me,[6] I gave assurances that I would continue to give myself away to the spirits so they could be my eyes and my feet and my wit, so I could see through their eyes, walk beside them and feel their presence making my continued journey a safe one.

I gradually returned to work, riding with Rosie every day because I could not drive. I was on heavy antiseizure medication, which kept me drowsy. Over the following twelve or so months, I tapered the medication down to one every two or three days with no complications, even though my neurologist had told me I would be on it for the rest of my life. In a conversation with Malidoma, however, he was clear that this problem was taken care of and I could discontinue it altogether. I did so with no bad effects.

The neurosurgeon was still puzzled about my case and asked me to see a number of other specialists at Tulane to try and put the pieces of this puzzle together. I never mentioned the spiritual interventions made for me by the medicine men. I was still new on the faculty and did not feel safe enough to chance sounding like a fool, nor did I feel the need to take such a risk.

At my six-month postoperative exam, my neurosurgeon requested another MRI of my brain. As I reviewed it with him, he shook his head and said, "This is a picture of a perfectly normal brain. This one sure fooled me." Thus I became the only one of all my relatives to have a certified normal brain. When one of my cousins called to check on me, I told her about it. She said, "Bring the X ray to the reunion, or no one'll believe it."

8

The Never-Ending Stories

*I*t took yet another six months for me to feel completely normal again, but at least I was able to work. Several men who had participated with us at DCI heard through the grapevine that I was sick and came by our offices to see how I was doing. Some of them were doing very well and some, including Andrew Webster (Psycho), signed up for the next class.

A dramatic change occurred with this new class. For the first time, women signed up for the program. I had doubts about mixed-gender groups. My concern was that the men would not be willing to go into their grief in the presence of women and that the women would not go as deeply into women's issues in the presence of men. In the indigenous world, the early stages of initiation are done separately, and for certain our work is with the uninitiated. But our small facility and all-male staff limited our ability to have separate groups, and if the men and women participants were to spend every day in class together, they should also build community with each other.

I immediately found, however, that my concerns were unsubstantiated. On the very first day of the community-building workshop, one woman took a great risk by talking about her experience of being raped. Another woman in the group, who had been raped numerous times as a child by her stepfather, related to the first woman's pain by speaking of her own. Within the next hour, almost every woman in the room who had been raped, which, tragically, was the majority, had gone down deep into the grief they had carried around for years. Another common thread that bound these women together was that, for nearly all of them, it was the first time they had ever told anyone about it. I remember wondering, *My God, what percentage of women in prison have been raped? And what percentage of those were raped as children?*

Something else happened in the room during that blessed hour: The men were also weeping over the women's pain. One of the women who shared her experience was a young white woman who was there as a volunteer literacy instructor. Expressing how deeply she was affected by the men's tears, she said, "I've talked about this before in groups of women, but this is the first time I've ever spoken about it in the presence of men, and it helps me to see men crying over this, because I thought they didn't care."

Then the men began to talk. One told the story of seeing his mother raped. The next man told of seeing his nine-year-old sister being raped by their uncle. As reality and realness continued to flow into the room, this group of men and women descended toward the bottom of this well of grief where they found trust, closeness and solidarity with each other. They would never look at each other quite the same again, and their worlds would never be quite as lonely as before. Passing each other on the street would never be as casual as before.

At the end of that first day of the workshop, I asked the participants if the group felt somehow different than it had when we began that morning. Calmly and solemnly they all nodded and said, "Yes."

——————

I decided the following September to invite three of our participants to the Minnesota Men's Conference. I reasoned that they would, in turn, spread the teachings of the conference to places where they might otherwise never reach. Without question, there have been instances in which participants who attended a conference brought the teachings back to their classmates at Project Return.

Another of my motivations for introducing the men of Project Return to the conferences was to spread what I had learned about prisons and "criminals" to other regions of the country in order to overcome some of the ignorance about who they are, and to encourage others that they are not powerless to effect dramatic changes in our culture and in the people whose lives they touch.

In September 1997, I asked a young man named Peyton Moore to represent his class at the Minnesota Men's Conference at Sturgeon Lake's Camp Miller. Peyton was one of the youngest men who had ever come to Project Return, and, at the time of his entry into the program, I had my doubts that he would complete the ninety-day course of activities and graduate. Like so many others when they are attending their first class in the program, Peyton looked at me with intense distrust. As always, I made it a point not to react to his glares or to take them personally, because I know that, for many nonwhite individuals, this is simply an ingrained reaction to anyone who is white—and is therefore a lifelong enemy. If this was the case with Peyton, my hope was, as always, that he would be able to openly talk about his stereotypical images of me and white people when the time came to do so.

Peyton did not let me down; in fact, he was an exemplary

participant in the community-building workshop that initiated his class for the ninety-day process at Project Return. He spoke eloquently about his tragic life, took risk after risk, and acted as a role model for his fifty classmates about what it means to get real, to open up and to let go of one's burdens of unspoken rage and grief. At one point during the second day of the workshop, he told us of the time he had "gone off" in prison and was strapped naked to a cement slab in the mental ward. The correctional officers left him there for two weeks, lying in his own urine and feces for days until someone bothered to hose him down. During this experience, he was terribly thirsty and begged the correctional officer to give him some water. The correctional officer threw the cup of water in his face.

As I listened to Peyton, I wept. When he was finished, I told him that I felt certain *I* would not have been able to survive such an ordeal. If the experience itself had not killed me, I probably would have killed myself afterwards. I told him, with all sincerity, that I wanted to learn what elements of character and soul provide some people with the endurance, resilience and courage not only to survive such an experience, but to be able to emerge from it as mentally and spiritually intact as he obviously was.

Something happened between us then—or, at least, began to happen. For me, this seemed like the beginning of another mentoring role, but one that was to be in no way ordinary. James Hillman describes these exceptional alliances between the mentor and the mentored as having two central require-ments. One, the student must be seen or perceived by the mentor, i.e., the mentor must be able to recognize the extraor-dinary characteristics of the young person that clearly reveal the essence, the longings and the *commands* of his soul—those tasks of living, learning and service that the soul charges us with in life. The other requirement is love. "Mentoring begins when your imagination can fall in love with the fantasy of another," Hillman claimed. The trouble, Hillman goes on to say, is that love between the mentor and the mentored tends to be seen in our culture "only with the genital eye as abuse, seduction, harassment or impersonal hormonal need."

For this reason, I am careful to describe the way I came to feel about Peyton, but I did come to admire and love him as a true mentor often does. My fantasy about Peyton was that he would become the Malcolm of his young generation at Project Return. I saw him as a leader in the juvenile compo-nent we were developing, inspiring young men to follow him along the path of integrity that he himself had chosen. He was also strikingly handsome, with solid black eyes that high-lighted his smiling face when he was learning something new, and he was like a sponge when it came to gathering and col-lecting new insights and awareness.

For all of these reasons, Peyton was my first choice that September 1997 to attend the Minnesota Men's Conference. A week of interaction with the positive male energy that always permeated these conferences would be the perfect reinforcement to all that he had harvested at Project Return. Furthermore, he would be a divine blessing to the conference, presenting an exemplary contradiction to the negative image most of us project onto convicted felons.

Two days before our flight to Minneapolis, and minutes before we were to go into our community-building session, I called Peyton's house to confirm final travel arrangements. His mother answered and informed me that he had been mistakenly shot to death two days before and that she had not known how to reach me. According to the young man who was with him, two gunmen opened fire on Peyton, hitting him seven times in the back. They ran up to him, rolled him over, and then one of them said to the other, "Dat ain't him," and they both ran off.

The vessel created by the circle of community fortunately was there to contain my grief as I informed the rest of the class of Peyton's death. One of the members of the circle said, "As sad as this is to me right now, I cannot help but recognize for the first time how much Bob loves and cares about us."

In the aftershock, I began to remember all the spiritualists, thinkers and philosophers I have read who said there are no accidents—that everything happens for a reason. I could not imagine that to be true in this case. What possible reason could there be for this extraordinary young man, who had such an exceptional potential for reclaiming lost souls, to be gunned down through mistaken identity? I wanted his murderers caught—not to be executed, but so they could be taken away to a place where they could not continue to render such harm to others. I also wanted somehow to lessen the harm they had brought.

I still held Peyton's ticket to the conference and began thinking that if the airline would allow us to change the name on the ticket, someone else could go in his place. That would, in a small manner, lessen the tragedy and maybe even some of the anguish I felt. I quickly consulted with Malcolm and we agreed to ask a young man named John La Fleur if he would like to go in Peyton's place.

John was profoundly grateful to be asked, and he accepted our invitation. I had not spent a lot of time with John during his participation at Project Return because he was white and I did not want to risk the appearance of racial favoritism. But I had received his letters from prison for a year before he joined us. John came to Project Return at the age of thirty-four after serving seventeen years in prison, thirteen of them in Camp J at Angola in an isolation cell. I heard that while he was in prison, an Episcopal priest took a special interest in him and worked with him during the latter years of his sentence. John was an excellent participant in our program, and I felt sure he would survive in free society even though he had not, in my opinion, gone very deep in what he disclosed about himself in the community sessions.

I was not in the same breakout group at the Men's Conference as he was, so we saw little of each other while we were there. I could tell, nonetheless, that he was excited to be there and that he was not shy about participating in activities and conversing with others. During one of the evening community sessions, he told the group about the circumstances that had led up to his attendance at the conference.

On the last day, with only about thirty minutes to go in the final session, Robert Bly asked the gathering if anyone had any last questions or things that they wanted to bring up. After a few seconds, an elderly gentleman stood up from his chair in the back of the room and proceeded to walk slowly toward the center aisle. I did not know who he was, nor could I remember ever having seen him before. As he continued to walk ever so slowly up the aisle toward the lecturer's platform, I wondered, *Now what does this guy want?* Arriving finally at the front of the room, he turned to face the assembly and said gently, in a saddened voice, "We must do something about prison rape. What can we do?" For the next few seconds, there was silence, and then Robert Moore of the University of Chicago Theological Seminary called upon me to come up to the microphone and answer the question.

I began my answer as I do when I am asked such questions by the media and only have limited time to respond. "There is no short answer to this question. It is a difficult and complex problem that requires a complex answer. But whenever

I'm forced to give a short answer, I say, 'Look in the mirror. Search your own life for the ways in which you hold some accountability for creating or perpetuating the problem, and then stop doing it. This might simply mean that you do not remain silent about a problem when there is an opportunity for you to speak out against it. I am not asking you to find out how you are to *blame*—that would be as useless as blaming someone else, which is what most of us do. But until you understand the role you have played in creating the problem, you will not be very effective in solving it.'"

I ended by giving the group some statistics and facts to illustrate the magnitude of the problem. I briefly explained that once a prisoner is raped, he is stigmatized and marked as a victim for repeated sexual assault for as long as he remains locked up, and that most victims are young, small, nonviolent and unable to defend themselves against ruthless exploitation. I gave them an estimate, relying on the findings of published systematic surveys of jails and prisons in America in 1994, that some 10,000 unwanted sexual acts take place behind bars in the United States every day, victimizing in the course of a year some 130,000 adult males in prisons, 30,000 in jails and 40,000 boys held in juvenile and adult facilities.

Full of rage and without the opportunity to receive psychological treatment for rape trauma syndrome, these men and boys will usually return to the community far more violent and antisocial than before they were raped. Some of them will perpetuate the vicious cycle by becoming rapists themselves in a misguided attempt to "regain their manhood" in the same manner in which they believe it was lost.

Then I called upon Malcolm to come up and present his standing on the matter. Malcolm told the group a story about an experience he had in jail. A young man had been thrown into the cell next to his with five other prisoners. Almost immediately, the five began to beat him into submission in order to gang rape him. Malcolm said that he knew each of the five men well, and that they respected him and would have stopped their attack if he had told them to do so. Instead, he followed the code that most prisoners live by: "It was not any of my business." Malcolm went on to describe the dreadful screams of a man being raped and told us that he had never forgotten it.

"This man's nightmare did not end that night, of course. Having been 'turned out' he was eventually 'claimed' by someone in the prison. From that point on, he was forced to repay his 'husband' for the violence inflicted upon him by devoting his existence to servicing his rapist's every need for years after."

Some fifteen years later, Malcolm had read in a newspaper brought to the prison that this same young man was about to be executed in Louisiana's electric chair for the rape and murder of his girlfriend's eleven-year-old girl.

Malcolm immediately wrote a letter to his friend Dr. Danesh, a political science professor at Southern University who had taught a free course at DCI. Over the years, the professor had become a trusted friend to Malcolm, whom he described as his most fervent student. Malcolm asked in his letter to Dr. Danesh if he would try to contact someone in authority to tell this man's story and show that, as always, there was more to the issue than the sole fact of his crime. The letter mysteriously took three weeks to travel thirty-five miles to Dr. Danesh's office. During that time, the young man was electrocuted in Angola's death house.

The gathering of men sat quietly as Malcolm finished his story and returned to his seat. It seemed enough had been said. The conference was at an end, or so I thought. All of a sudden, John La Fleur walked to the front of the room, faced the group and began to speak in a voice that was tight with emotion.

"When I was seventeen, I was serving time in a juvenile facility in Baton Rouge, where the judge had sent me on the condition that I behave myself for two years. If I didn't, he was gonna charge me as an adult and send me to Angola for thirty years. One day, I blew off at one of the counselors 'cause I thought he had been screwing me over. That same day, he had me moved into one of the dormitories that housed only black kids. That night, I was attacked, tied to the end of a bed, and raped by all twenty-five of them. Within weeks of that night, I was moved to Angola where I spent the next seventeen years. For thirteen of those years, I was kept at a place called Camp J, which is a maximum-security camp that had isolation cells, but I was there by choice. I kept acting up so bad because I was afraid for them to put me in the population. You see, once you been what they call 'turned out' . . ."

Although we were in Minnesota, John was nevertheless taking a considerable risk in recounting his experience in the juvenile prison. There were other participants from our program in the room. What if they betrayed the confidentiality that is part of such meetings? If John were ever returned to prison for a technical error in his parole process, which happens on occasion, and if word ever reached the prison population that he had been turned out in the juvenile system, he could be subjected to the same codes of prison conduct as anyone else.

John finished telling his story. He returned to his seat, put his head in his hands and began to sob, his body trembling. The room was silent for a while. Then a grief chant quietly began, allowing his weeping to continue for as long as he needed.

For as long as I had known John, I had seen that he was harboring a terrible secret. I could see it in his eyes, hear it in his voice and in the words that he shared with the group, words that never quite completed the passionate release that people commonly feel when they have unloaded their burdens of brokenness and shame. Following the conference, I could clearly see that a tremendous healing had occurred in John—and it had all begun because one lone person had seized the opportunity to stand up and declare the truth.

David Whyte says,

Loaves and Fishes

*This is not
the age of information.*

This is not
the age of information.

*Forget the news,
and the radio,
and the blurred screen.*

*This is the time
of loaves
and fishes.*

*People are hungry,
and one good word is bread
for a thousand.*

The next spring, while several of us were reminiscing about our times at DCI, Andrew Webster (formerly Psycho) asked Malcolm and me if we had heard anything about Larry Brown and Bubba Sanders. Malcolm said Larry had relapsed on drugs, but had admitted himself to a state recovery center in Mandeville and was, for the time being, doing well. I had kept up with Bubba for about a year after he left Hope House in Baton Rouge. He had been arrested for possession and use of marijuana, but he was also charged with being in a car with another convicted felon. After six months or so in the parish jail, he left Baton Rouge to live with his grandmother near Lafayette. The last time I had spoken with him, he was going to Alcoholics Anonymous meetings regularly and had a good sponsor and a decent job. But I had no recent news. The last time I'd called his grandmother's number to check on Bubba, the service had been disconnected with no forwarding number.

Since we'd heard nothing from either of them for awhile, we agreed that Malcolm would look up Larry and I would find Bubba. I remembered that Bubba's full name was Hardy Sanders Jr., so I began an Internet search for his father. Mr. Sanders remembered me and was glad to give me Bubba's number. It was about 7:30 in the evening when I called Bubba. His voice sounded terrible as he asked me to hang on while he took the cordless phone outside so we could talk in private. He began crying in disbelief that I had called on this of all nights, the night he intended to commit suicide by overdosing on cocaine. The woman he lived with was a cocaine dealer from whom he could get enough dope to kill himself. He explained that he had fallen deep into debt to someone whom he could not repay. Apparently, this person said that if Bubba would help him burglarize a tobacco store, he would forgive the debt. In doing so, however, they had set off the alarm and were caught, leaving Bubba to face another prison term of five years.

Sobbing, Bubba added, "And, Bob, I think I have AIDS." I asked him why he thought so. He said he had slept with a woman who later told him she was HIV-positive. Bubba had gone to Charity Hospital in Baton Rouge and was tested, but the results would be a month in coming back. He said, "Bob, I go for sentencing next week. There ain't time to find out. An' Bob, I don't want to die in prison. I don't want to die there."

That's every prisoner's worst nightmare, I thought. I told Bubba that if he could catch a bus to New Orleans the next morning, I would have him tested at Tulane's blood lab and find out the results the next afternoon. Then he and I made a contract that he would not overdose, at least until after the test result was in. The next morning, his father drove him down for the test. Afterward, I took them to lunch and Bubba filled me in on events surrounding the burglary charge.

Bubba had already confessed to the crime. All that remained was to get the judge to agree to give him a shorter sentence and avoid a trial. The problem, however, was that the court could not find a public defender who could take the case and bargain for him, since they were already overloaded with cases. A black lawyer who overheard the proceedings in the courtroom had "nobly" volunteered to take the case for free. However, when he found out that Bubba *really* had no money, he made himself scarce. The prosecutor had set five dates for a meeting to bargain Bubba's sentence, but the lawyer had kept none of them. Finally, the prosecutor told Bubba that, by law, he had to be represented by a lawyer when deciding the length of sentence, but if Bubba would cooperate with him, he would go easy on him. Together, they agreed on five years, which was truly a bargain, because this was Bubba's fourth offense, and the district attorney had the option to bill him as a habitual offender and send him to prison for life. Since there was no way to sentence him in court without the presence of a legal representative, the judge issued a bench warrant for the lawyer's arrest to get him in court on the day of Bubba's sentencing.

I told Bubba and his father that I would call them the next afternoon when I got the results of his blood test. I also told them that I would try and talk to the judge.

The next morning I had to leave for a two-day conference at the University of Chicago that focused on Project Return. Since the conference did not start until that evening, and two of my sons lived in Chicago at that time, I met them for lunch at Berghof's, a well-known German restaurant. After ordering, I went to the pay phone and called the lab for the test results. Since my name was on the slip as the person who had ordered the test, the technician was able to tell me the results—negative for HIV. I immediately hung up and called Bubba with the good news. We agreed that he would continue to hang in there until I could talk with the judge about his case. When I reached the judge that afternoon, he told me that I could talk to him early on the day of the hearing.

I arrived very early that morning, hoping to see the judge in his chambers rather than in the courtroom. Judge Richard Arnaud was a pleasant, balding man in his mid-forties who looked dreadfully burned out. He graciously gave me enough time to put forward a synopsis of Bubba's story, of how he had been institutionalized and mistreated since the age of six. I finished by telling him what I could do for Bubba at Project Return.

Judge Arnaud said, "You know, I like this young man, and you know why—because he's so honest. I've had him in my court before and he's always respectful, he always tells the truth and he's always so sorry for screwing up again. And I'd like to help him out. But he's already pled guilty and plea-bargained his sentence with the prosecutor—and he made out pretty well, given his record. So, right now, this whole thing is in the prosecutor's hands. You can talk to him, but it's awfully late in the game to be trying to change *his* mind."

At this point, Bubba's lawyer, Floyd Jackson, sheepishly walked in and sat down. Judge Arnaud introduced him to me and told him why I was there. The judge then agreed to invite the prosecutor in so I could take my best shot with him. I quickly went out into the hallway of the courtroom where Bubba was waiting and brought him up-to-date. As I turned to go back into the judge's chambers, Bubba's prosecutor, Stan Brock, stepped off the elevator. When Floyd saw Brock, he blurted out, "Say, I hear we're gonna get my client off." At this point, Stan started yelling at the man, sounding for all the world like a barking dog, "Don't even think for one god-damn second you're gonna waltz in here an' . . ."

This tirade continued all the way into Judge Arnaud's office, and I figured we were dead in the water. I waited for the prose-cutor to stop yelling before I joined them. Judge Arnaud intro-duced me to Stan, who was sitting on a couch to the judge's right, his eyes red with anger. I remembered a rule of conflict from the Aikido martial arts that one should try to see his enemy's point of view. I took my seat next to the young prosecutor so that we would be looking at the room from the same perspective.

When Judge Arnaud and I told the prosecutor Bubba's story, he looked over at me and asked, "And what do you think you can do with this guy?" I told him that if I could get him into Project Return for ninety days, I believed I could sta-bilize him enough to get him a job on an offshore oil rig. When Stan looked back at me, his eyes were still red, but now they were also wet. He said, "You know, I actually like this kid. He has never tried to bullshit me and he's been so apologetic that I've wanted to help him."

Stan then turned to Judge Arnaud and said, "You know, Judge, Mr. Sanders and I bargained this sentence without legal representation. If Bubba chose to appeal that, he would win. So I'm willing to drop the felony charge if we can charge him with something else to get him on probation so he'll have to go with Dr. Roberts and stay with him. What can we use?"

With a slight grin on his face, Judge Arnaud said, "Well, we've never used bear wrestling before." The room fell apart with laughter.

"Great," Stan said. "What else have you got?"

"Well, there's actually a law that specifically prohibits the theft of crawfish," said the judge.

The joking and laughter continued, but suddenly it hit me that the system had actually begun to function the way in which it was intended. Bubba had never harmed anyone, so the public's safety was not an issue. What would five more years in a Louisiana prison do for him? Everyone knew he would emerge even more crippled than he already was.

I thought for a moment about what Malidoma had told me happens when taboos are broken in the indigenous world. The elders would have said to Bubba, "You have separated yourself from the ways of our village and, if you have to leave, then you will take away the gift you brought with you, and the village will be less than it was. Therefore, what can we do that will help you to rejoin our village and fulfill your purpose in coming to us?" So, Bubba was not being sent away.

As my thoughts came back to the room, the laughter was subsiding—the final charge mentioned had something to do with donut holes. Then Judge Arnaud turned to me and asked if I thought I could talk Bubba into accepting the new charges and pleading guilty to them. He was serious!

Moments later, I was choking back the laughter as I sat in the courtroom listening to the black-robed Judge Arnaud read the charges as soberly as any man could.

"Mr. Sanders, you've been duly charged with bear wrestling within the city limits of Baton Rouge. How do you plead?"

"Guilty, Your Honor," Bubba replied.

"Mr. Sanders, you've also been charged with the misdemeanor theft of crawfish. How do you plead?" And so it went. Judge Arnaud told Bubba that he would have to go to New Orleans and remain under my supervision until graduation from Project Return. He would remain under my supervision for the next two years. If at any time . . . , etc., etc., etc. Moments later, Bubba and I were headed for New Orleans to find him a place to stay.

The next morning when I walked into the office with Bubba, Malcolm congratulated me on "winning my first case." Since then, I have been amazed at how many judges have released people into my custody, or simply let them out of jail when I gave them reason to do so. I have found there are many judges who are sick of sending people to jail over and over, and they are desperately looking for anyone who will offer viable options. That was a crucial factor I had added to the equation in Bubba's case that is all too often missing—a sentencing alternative.

Though Bubba continued to hit every bump in the road, he finished the program and graduated. We discovered that his weakness for getting high was equaled only by his weakness for women in distress. He has managed to stay off drugs but has tried to rescue half a dozen women who were living through the same crises that Bubba experienced, and they have taken his money every time. That next September, I took him with me to the Minnesota Men's Conference to give him the experience of hanging out with serious, eloquent, positive, wounded and zany older men. While there, he wrote a poem that astonished everyone with its eloquence.

Angels—seem to be always within distance.
They hear when I weep and can sense the danger around the corner
Even when I am blind to it.
What are their names?
I want to know so much about them.
Time after time they rescue me from the steel jaws of death,
Even when his teeth are in the very mirror of my existence.
Why me?
Who am I to deserve such guardians,
After creating so much chaos and living in so much deceit?

I have lived with that question hanging from the cobwebs of
My mind for so long, hardly even giving thanks.
I live in so much fear of it because I never could grasp an
Understanding of it.
But today I have no choice but to know it exists and is at work
Carrying me through life and loving me even when I am hating
Myself.
Yet today, I can no longer take it with a grain of salt.
Today, I want to know my angels so I can talk with them, embrace
Them, sing to them, and give them thanks. So much thanks!

Hardy Sanders Jr.

Following his graduation, we were not able to get Bubba the
job on the oil rig, as I had promised Judge Arnaud. A previous
injury to his neck prevented him from passing the physical
exam. I was disappointed. The job would have offered him
benefits far beyond the usual ones, such as a structured, calm
environment (being over the water). With clothing, entertain-
ment, room and board, good pay, drug testing, and ample time
ashore, it would have provided him with the perfect halfway
house. Concerned that an ordinary job on the streets did not
offer him the structure he still needed, Judge Arnaud permitted
Bubba to leave the state and enroll in a "recovery" farm in
Georgia. The farm work, done in the mornings, was followed
by addictions recovery work in the afternoon and evening.

Before long, Bubba called to tell me that he had become

one of the counselors. The last time he called, he said that his
life was going better than it ever had. He completed his
course at the farm and moved up to North Carolina to be near
his brother Troy, an auto mechanic. Bubba found a good job
loading trucks and had his own apartment, his own telephone
and an old Ford that Troy fixed up for him. "But," he told me,
"I'm scared to death. I'm so scared I'm gonna screw it up and
lose it all, because that's what I've always done before."

"What do you think could be lying underneath this recur-
ring fear?" I asked.

He answered, "The toughest thing for me to believe is that
I deserve all this." For Bubba, the road will still have its
bumps and potholes, but for the time being, a sad and troubling story has ended well.

Knowing the whole story, I think most people would agree
that it has also ended *justly*. But knowing the whole story is
crucial to arrive at that conclusion. Without it, we would have
been left only with the facts on Bubba's rap sheet. These would
have merely shown a lengthy succession of numerous brushes
with the law,[†] and left most of us to conclude that a judge and

---

[†] "Brushes with the Law" are dreary, repetitive crises in the dismal, dreary life of
one of the "miserable ones." They are signals of distress, signals of failure, signals
of crises which society sees primarily in terms of its annoyance, its irritation, its
injury. They are the spasms and struggles and convulsions of a human being psychology calls submarginal, who is trying to make it in our complex society with
inadequate equipment and inadequate preparation.

"Brushes are exemplified by: (a) repetitive arrests and incarcerations, but with a prosecutor had allowed a habitual offender to get off lightly. Yet, we know that since Bubba was six years old (and probably even before that), he has never gotten off lightly.

Karl Menninger, in *The Crime of Punishment*, said that such "whole stories" are of no interest to the law.

> *Why the impulse to break the law becomes so powerful as to elude all the existing controls, internal and external, is of no interest to the law or most representatives of the law. What various forces combine to determine a particular antisocial illegal act—this is no concern of the law. How internal pressures and external events lead up to the criminal act as a logical link in a continuing chain of behavior and adaptation—this is not a legal question nor a legal concern.*
>
> *The law is concerned only with the fact that its stipulations were broken, and the one who breached them must be officially and socially hurt (punished). Then everything will be all right*

no constructive response to the personality disturbance that must underlie the accumulation of transgressions; (b) the minimizing of serious threats to the safety of the innocent; and, (c) the inflation to unbelievable proportions minor pieces of delinquency.

"Brushes cost the city and the state a good deal of money, keep a good many people busy doing the prescribed but futile things that the law calls for. They spell agony and despair and failure for one guy—a "worthless" guy to some—but a human being. What an exercise in futility to arrest him, sentence him, lock him up a while, and then loose him into the current again and let him try to swim.

—*Karl Menninger*

> *again—"justice" will have been done. When such instances of*
> *lawbreaking can be seen as pieces in a total pattern of*
> *appalling abuse and powerlessness, one ceases even to wonder*
> *why or how.*

In this case, we can say that Judge Arnaud and Assistant District Attorney Brock were more interested in Bubba's whole story than in the letter of the law, which often is all these two men have to work with. Had they considered only the law, would justice have been served? Perhaps so, but what about the public safety? Sentencing Bubba to five more years of imprisonment could have at last turned him into a violent criminal.

I have come to dislike hearing the word "justice," and I'm not in bad company. Oliver Wendell Holmes did not like hearing it either. In fact, Justice Holmes was known to admonish a lawyer whose argument before the Supreme Court was based on the term "justice." He said it showed the lawyer was shirking his job. He said that justice is a subjective, emotional word so vague, so distorted in its applications, so hypocritical and usually so irrelevant that it offers no help in the solution of the crime problem that it exists to combat. Furthermore, he said that it does not advance a solution to use the word "justice," but that the problem in every case is what should be done in *this* situation. "Whether it is shoplifting or violent assault, these are behaviors which must be controlled, discouraged, and stopped; but these," according to Holmes, "are matters of public safety, not justice. The question is not what would be just to do to this dangerous fellow or that dishonest woman, but what will lead them to react more acceptably and will protect the environment in the meantime."

This is what the current system based on the concepts of justice and precedent fails to do. As a result, many young men and women whom we have labeled as dangerous criminals, like Bubba, languish away in our prison system, which is troubling. Perhaps they would not be there had *their stories* come to light. Yes, there are some who are beyond our help, and public safety would be jeopardized if they were released. But I have learned that these individuals make up a small percentage of our prison population. Moreover, mandatory sentencing laws, which prevent judges from considering "the whole story" in sentencing, have worsened the problem. I do not imply that people should not be held accountable for their actions; but accountability, by my definition of the word, must be shared.

I recently came across a prime example of this. A seventeen-year-old boy in Texas was sentenced to prison and labeled for life as a sex offender for sleeping with a thirteen-year-old girl. According to the story, the girl admittedly told the boy she was fifteen the night she sneaked out of the house to meet him, and she also admitted that the sex was consensual. For the rest of his life, however, the boy must remain registered as a sex offender and have his picture on a sex-offender Web site for the world to see.

This type of story, where the most fundamental and essential understanding of children's behavior gets completely ignored, happens thousands of times a day in juvenile courts across the country. The understanding is that children learn their behavior from the adult world, not from their own. Although psychologists are very clear about this, we descend on our children with extreme prejudice for emulating us in ways that we do not like.

The indigenous cultures around the world, which we call primitive, understand this concept very well. Martín Prechtel taught me that in the Mayan culture, the children are called the "conscience of the village." This means that when the children become upset, disruptive or violent, the elders come together and ask themselves, "What are *we* doing wrong that our children are becoming violent? And what do *we* need to change about ourselves that will restore their harmony with the village?"

Think for a moment how analogous the behaviors of the young boy and girl in Texas are to that of former President Bill Clinton and Monica Lewinsky. Yet the law in Texas, which was written to protect the populace from true pedophiles, was imposed in such a way that it placed all blame on the young man. When we do this, our culture is weakened because we have failed to examine our own accountability, and nothing changes.[†] Even though Bill Clinton was impeached for his behavior, during his trial numerous reporters estimated that two-thirds of the members of Congress are guilty of living the same kind of lifestyle as the former president.

The Juvenile Awareness Project Help (JAPH), a well-known study that spawned the Academy Award–winning documentary film *Scared Straight*, illustrated the unquestionable process by which children learn their behavior. This study was highly publicized nationwide in the media as the miracle cure for juvenile delinquency—that is, until the real results of the study were discovered.

The architects of the program selected a population of young boys and divided them into two types of groups: control groups, which consisted of boys who stayed at home; and treatment groups, which consisted of boys who were taken into prisons where prisoners loudly and aggressively shouted terrorizing remarks at them, ranging from threats of rape to threats of plucking a boy's eye out and squishing it in front of him. This experience was supposed to frighten the boys so much that they would be "scared straight."

[†] "Equity bids us be merciful to the weakness of human nature; to think less about the laws than about the man who framed them, and less about what he said than what he meant; not to consider the actions of the accused so much as his intentions, nor this nor that detail so much as the *whole* story; to ask not what a man is now but what he has always or usually been."

—*Aristotle*

When researchers from Rutgers University evaluated the program several years later, they discovered that the treatment groups did much worse than the controls. Out of one treatment group containing nineteen kids *with no prior record,* six were arrested within the next six months. Out of twenty-one kids in one of the control groups (those who did not receive the "treatment"), all who also had no prior record, only one was subsequently arrested. Why? For one thing, the program did not really get at the *root causes of crime.* In no way did it address poverty, ramshackle schools, poor families and broken homes, jobless summers, or racial discrimination, which are the real causes of juvenile crime and delinquency. Furthermore, given that children learn their behavior from the adult world, the treatment group that visited the prisons learned firsthand that our government responds to brutality with more brutality. Might they have also learned that if you have enemies it is okay to hate them and harm them?

One of the most glaring examples of this came about during the shootings at Columbine High School in Littleton, Colorado. At one point during the television broadcast of the tragedy as it was still unfolding, Aaron Kipnis, the well-known author of *Angry Young Men,* heard a CNN reporter ask, "How can children from good families have such callous disregard for human life?" Suddenly, the network cut to a breaking story in Kosovo about an Air Force fighter jet that had unintentionally destroyed a railroad bridge while a passenger train was crossing it. The scene was a press conference in which an Air Force general referred to the deaths of the 150 civilian passengers on the train as "collateral damage." Unwittingly, the network had divulged a primary source of such callous disregard for human life. If the leaders of our country feel such disregard for the lives of our enemies, then how will our children feel about the lives of their enemies?

My intention in creating Project Return was to speak to the very question of blame versus accountability by asking, "As a society, in what way do we hold some accountability for the fact that so many of our people repeat over and over again the cycle of drugs, crime, violence and imprisonment? And what do we need to change about ourselves that would help them to break these cycles?" One answer to the first question is that we return offenders to the streets more traumatized and sociopathic than when they first entered prison because of the violence our prison system ignores and/or condones.

For an effective program of making the offender suffer by beating him to his knees, there must be unassailable power ranged against him, otherwise he will rise up in his vengeance and pay us back. He will do a little punishing according to his lights . . . and his vengeance is always turned against those nearest at hand and least prepared for the onslaught. "They that live by the sword shall die by the sword" is what we were taught; but were never have believed it. So long as the spirit of vengeance has the slightest vestige of respectability, so long as it pervades the public mind and infuses the statute books of the law, we will make no headway toward the control of crime. Nor can we assess the most appropriate [treatment and] effective penalties so long as we seek to inflict retaliatory pain.

KARL MENNINGER

Furthermore, most convicted felons enter prison and leave prison with a fourth-grade education, a monkey on their back (addiction), no real job experience, no marketable skills and a battered sense of worth.

Judge Dennis A. Challeen, in his book *The NORP Think Factor*, offered his opinion on the subject of our "rehabilitative" methods.

We want offenders to have self-worth, so we destroy their self-worth. We want them to be responsible, so we take away all responsibilities. We want them to learn to be part of our community, so we isolate them from our community. We want them to be kind and loving people, so we subject them to hate and cruelty. We want them to quit being the tough guy, so we put them where the tough guy is respected. We want them to stop hanging around losers, so we put all the losers in one state under the same roof. We want them to be positive and constructive, so we degrade them and make them useless. We want them to be trustworthy, so we put them where there is no trust. We want them to be nonviolent, so we put them where there is violence all around them. We want them to quit exploiting us, so we put them where they exploit each other. We want them to take control of their lives, own their problems and stop being a parasite, so we make them totally dependent on us.

For nine years, Project Return has struggled to answer for society's accountability in creating this revolving prison door. During this time, we have become one of the best-known and most respected prison-to-community programs in the nation and the only one funded by the U.S. Department of Justice. To demonstrate and prove the effectiveness of our cutting-edge technology, we needed a stringent outside evaluation. The New Orleans Metropolitan Crime Commission conducted such an investigation, which showed remarkable outcomes with regard to reducing recidivism and violence. This evaluation showed that we saved the taxpayers a great deal of money. Our program generated a 40:1 return-on-investment ratio by creating $209 million in savings to taxpayers and victims of crime on a $5 million investment over five years. We accomplished this by reducing recidivism from the average rate of 75 percent among the "control population," which did not attend Project Return, to an average of 25 percent for our graduates over the four years studied.

We didn't achieve this success by accepting only the "cream," those former offenders who stood the best chance of survival in the outside world. On the contrary, our acceptance policy is to serve those with the greatest need, those who are at greatest risk of returning to prison. In other words, we take the "worst" applicants, such as those who have already relapsed on drugs, returned to dealing drugs, robbed or burglarized, or carry a gun. These go to the head of the line because they are the ones we want off the streets. And we want them off the streets not for another five years of prison time but once and for all. Of the eight hundred Project Return graduates studied, 40 percent had been convicted for violent crimes prior to attending Project Return. Less than 6 percent of the 25 percent who returned to prison did so for a violent crime.

These wonderful accomplishments, however, in no way compensate for all the causes of crime nor do they present a panacea for them. Our country must take a hard look in the mirror and then reverse the policies and practices that continually marginalize the poor and minorities through lack of opportunity, dilapidated inner-city schools and our reliance on imprisonment to solve the problems these conditions present.

There is one very important thing that must be understood about Project Return and why it has been successful. The grief work that we call community building, which we developed from Dr. M. Scott Peck's model, is the foundation of everything we do, including education and recovery from addiction. In reality, though, this is not a new technology. Community building has been around as long as human cultures have existed on the planet. It works so naturally and so effectively because it is so ancient. It lives in us as something that can and needs to be remembered. To learn it, then, is not to memorize a new system of procedures, but to remember something we once knew but forgot. Psychologist Robert Moore calls this something our "hard wiring."

In every indigenous culture, grief was part of the initiatory rites (passages) that led the youth into responsible adulthood. For men, it was important to learn how to grieve before one learned to be a warrior. What modern psychology teaches today the ancient elders have known for millennia: that repressed emotions will always return in distorted and monstrous forms. Grief, for instance, often returns as depression, but more often, it returns as rage, which is altogether different from anger.

Tribal elders understood that childhood is wounding, and that if a young man was not helped to grieve the wounds of his childhood, he would likely carry them around in his body as rage, thus making him dangerous to other people. Therefore, before he could safely be taught to use a weapon, those wounds of childhood had to be healed, leaving him with only the scars. In some cultures of Africa, the young initiate would receive a ceremonial wound on his shoulder that would develop into a scar others could see. Thus, when he chanced upon another warrior in the bush and each saw the other's scar, each would know he was in the presence of a safe person because, through the initiatory experience of grief, each had brought closure to the pain and suffering of his own childhood.

Remember that Robert Bly put this another way at the Minnesota conference. He said that the young boy who has been initiated will still erupt into the world as a dangerous man, but he will be a danger to racism, sexism, the pollution of the Earth and other evils. He will be willing to become violent, but only if the well-being of his family or village is threatened. He will never kill for material wealth or to sustain the price of oil.

The word "violence," according to Thomas Moore, comes from the Latin word *vis*, meaning "life force." "Its very roots," Moore says, "suggest that, in violence, the thrust of life is making itself visible. It would be a mistake to approach violence with any simple idea of getting rid of it. Chances are, if we try to eradicate our violence, we will also cut ourselves off from the deep power that sustains creative life. Besides, as psychoanalysis teaches, repression never accomplishes what we want. The life current of the soul, *vis*, is like the natural force of plant life, like the grass that grows up through cement and in a relatively short time obliterates grand monuments of culture. If we try taming and boxing in this innate power, it will inevitably find its way into the light, often in a destructive form."

At one of the Men's Conferences, Michael Meade gave

us an amazing analogy from the Masai of East Africa. Their name for this life force is *Latima*—that violent emotion peculiar to the masculine part of things that is the source of quarrels, ruthless competition, possessiveness, power-drivenness, ambition and brutality. But it is also the source of independence, courage, upstandingness, wildness rather than savagery, high emotions, ideals (true idealism comes from the same place as brutality), the movement towards individuation and the very source of the desire for initiation.

Martín and Malidoma taught us that their cultures honor this energy when it makes its appearance and teach their young men, through initiation, how to harness and polish it. This means today that when a man is beating his wife, he is not being overly masculine, he's being too boyish—because he has never been given a harness for this violent energy. It also means that he is still carrying in his body the residual shame and rage from the wounds of his childhood.

According to Meade, "How *Latima* happens, whether it becomes constructive or destructive, is the responsibility of older men and is the reason for initiation." However, as Bly points out, city culture, or human culture as we know it, attempts only to dampen this aggressive drive in children by taboos, rules, parental tyranny, religious doctrine, threats of exile (prison), hellfire and/or beatings that usually take place in the family or the school.

Finally, Robert Moore reminds us, in his book *King, Warrior, Magician, Lover,* of the "soft, spiritual male" in the sixties and seventies whose emotions were never activated at all because they were afraid of this aggressive, eruptive energy and would not own it. "It was often in these men that we found depression, reticence, hiding and lethargy which came out of a moral decision not to erupt into the world and become dangerous. So, they were not dangerous to women; but they were also not a danger to oppression, racism, pollution or sexual harassment." Moore adds, "Their women did not like them either and their divorce rate remained high."

For a long period of time, the more I learned about initiation, the more my frustration grew that we can never go back to those indigenous ways of bringing our young into true adulthood. In his perspective of initiation in the West, however, Malidoma gives me hope that our efforts in community building as grief work have placed Project Return on the right course. In his book *The Healing Wisdom of Africa,* Malidoma tells the hypothetical story of a man's fall from success in business and society that results in a prison sentence, parole and starting his life over again.

He cites this man's experience as an example in every way of a true initiation. "It just doesn't have the formality of an indigenous initiation. But initiation," he says, "is intimately connected to ordeal." From the indigenous point of view, our ordeals stretch the physical self far enough to bring about more awareness, more sense of responsibility, more wisdom and more discipline, which aims us toward the knowledge that we are going somewhere purposeful in life.

However, Malidoma points out that the immediate issue for us in this country is not finding initiatory experiences (trouble), but rather, it is how to bring closure to the pain and suffering that results from them. Many people with whom I have worked have tried to forget or somehow seal off an initiatory experience so that they can get on with something else, and it has been difficult for them to learn that it just doesn't work that way.

The problem is that in order for such suffering to pass, it has to be recognized. "It is the absence of radical and genuine recognition and acknowledgment that makes suffering grow larger," Malidoma writes. "The initiatory experience and the suffering that accompanies it end when the person's suffering has been acknowledged by others. Radical recognition takes place when a community witnesses the hardship being endured by a person, or the wounds he or she suffered."

The village where Malidoma comes from recognizes the suffering of the initiated boys upon their return home by turning out en masse to acknowledge the ordeal they have endured. And the greater the number of people witnessing and acknowledging the suffering, the better for them, since "an ordeal that has not been witnessed and acknowledged is likely to repeat itself."

There is an endless series of unresolved initiations in the

modern world due to the isolationism we practice, and our troubles, therefore, become personalized. "In addition," Malidoma says, "there is a tendency for many to ostracize people who seek to have their suffering acknowledged. The psyche of a person who seeks recognition as a way to end the suffering from an initiation experience interprets this ostracism as a sign that the world hasn't noticed, so it sends a message to repeat the experience in hopes that next time someone will notice."

At Project Return, we attempt to harness the violent emotions brought from childhood and prison by recognizing and acknowledging our clients' suffering in the community-building groups. Once participants descend into their grief, in front of fifty to seventy-five witnesses, they tend to find a way through and past the pain and discover what is underneath it: their ability to reason and think their way through difficulty and conflict.

Without such practices in the modern world, we are left with a society of people trying to function in a rational way and trying to find happiness and fulfillment while walking around in bodies full of grief and rage. When Western cultures abandoned the practice of initiation, much of the understanding of grief work was lost and we spent the next thousand or so years developing ways to disguise it. Therefore, when this grief erupted in distorted and monstrous forms of rage, we found only distorted and monstrous ways of dealing with it.[†] Of equal importance is that these modern-day eruptions are not limited to violence, crime and drug addictions in the streets. They also manifest as corruption in the highest levels of politics and in the corporate world as massive layoffs in conjunction with 500 percent increases in salaries at executive levels.

Evidence abounds that drug use, violence and criminal activity are found in *all* segments of society. The wealthy and privileged share the same ignorance about grieving childhood wounds as any other segment of modern culture. The disproportionate populations that occupy our prisons, including our death rows, only reflect the ability of the wealthy to pay for good lawyers and judges who impose "justice" according to race and class (although this is, at times, done unwittingly).

Today, for example, the FBI is training school principals to "profile" potentially violent children, but these profiles do not include the "A" student who will climb to the top of the corporate ladder and commit serious white-collar offenses, such as those at Enron. With his own rage stored somewhere in his body, his choice of weapons will become his briefcase, and his ammunition will be a sell-off of personal stock or a downsizing plan that destroys the future of twenty-two thousand people purely for the sake of personal or investor profit.

[†] Today, as third-world cultures abandon their indigenous practices of initiation, we can observe the eruption of violent behaviors not previously known to them.

Beyond doing grief work and harnessing this violent life force, we make a great effort at Project Return to incorporate that part of initiation that sees and honors the gift each person brings to this life. In the indigenous world, this teaching is based on the simple concept that each of us has a soul. Throughout the millennia, cultures have believed in the existence of the soul. They have also believed that the soul comes here from another place—for instance, the spirit world or heaven—and that it comes here for a reason or purpose, which is our unique gift.

Cultures have always had the belief that on the way here, or during infancy, we forget what that purpose is. James Hillman, in *The Soul's Code*, tells of an ancient Hebrew story in which an angel touches each of us in the middle of our upper lip as we are leaving the Hall of Souls and says, "Shhh, you won't remember this." That is why, the story says, we have an indentation in our upper lip, and that is also why we often put our finger there when trying to remember something.

Throughout the indigenous world, the primary purpose of initiation, beyond the work of grieving and harnessing our emotional and violent energies, is the ritual process of remembering who we are and why we came. Can you imagine what the world would be like if everyone knew by the age of fourteen who they were and why they were here? If indeed we do have souls, it represents a great failure of Western culture that the question of who we are and why we are here is either never asked or that it requires fifty years to answer instead of fourteen. That is how great leaders wind up never running for president, how poets wind up on academic committees, how spiritual healers wind up in dentistry and how men like Dan Quayle wind up in the White House.

On this subject, Martín Prechtel says that in the Mayan culture, the boy must first marry his soul before he is ready to marry a woman. Bly says that when this does not happen, a man will look for his soul in a woman. I have asked many groups of men what feelings accompanied the times they fell in love, and their answers always include that sense of wholeness and completeness. I personally found that the ecstasy and sense of wholeness I had when I finally connected with my soul felt incredibly similar to the times I had fallen in love. No wonder we get so mixed up. Perhaps this difference between being connected with the soul and looking for our soul in another person defines the difference between *wanting* as opposed to *needing* a partner. The women in my classes at Project Return and at Tulane have always said they could tell the difference between a man who wanted them and a man who needed them.

My meager efforts at helping former prisoners remember their souls have been limited to teaching the basic elements of meditative practice. It was through such practices that I first felt the joy and love that I believe came from my soul. However, meditation is the most difficult of all the practices

I offer former offenders in the part of the program known as the development of life skills. "The difficulty," they tell me, "is that every time I get quiet, all I hear is screaming." Once when Martín sat with us in the circle, a community member told him that he was having terrible nightmares about going back to prison and asked, "How do I keep my nightmares from coming true?" Martín answered, "You tell the whole village." So I ask them to bring their screams to the community, to share them and try again.

The most important thing to remember about initiation is that, like grief, it never ends. Once initiates learn the art of grieving, harness the life force of aggression and remember their reasons for coming here, they become initiated into responsibility for others. They transform into the spiritual guides who lead younger initiates through their rites of passage. Today, there is a cry for mentors to work with troubled youth, many of whom come from fatherless or motherless homes.

At Project Return, we decided that both staff and participants would endeavor to be accountable to the youth of New Orleans through mentorship. Like grief work, mentorship has been around as long as cultures have existed on the planet. It is the bridge on the lifelong path of initiation over which one crosses into eldership. Therefore, our desire to be mentored is as hardwired as our need to grieve. In the indigenous world, where everyone has come with a gift, the job of the mentor is to help the young boy or girl to recognize the qualities of this gift and begin to trust it. Mentorship is not exactly a teacher/student relationship, however. This is where many of the mentoring programs around the country, even some I have visited that are referred to as "Afro-centric," plainly miss the mark. In such programs, the mentor plays the role of worthy adviser who assumes, as our educational system does, that the child's head is an empty vessel that needs to be filled with what adults know. The true mentorship role is one of seeing and praising the gift, the genius, that is in every young person.

The mentors we train at Project Return might say, when asked for advice, "Look, I'm just as lost as you. The only difference between us is that I've been lost longer. That only means that I've tried some of the paths that lie before you. Some that I thought would lead me towards manhood didn't. If you want to hear what I found, you may ask, but I can only give you my own experience. I won't tell you how to live your life." If a former offender had mentored Clarence Williams[†], he might not have believed that "prison is where you go to become a man." Perhaps a well-trained mentor would have said, "I only found death there."

A dramatic experience of mentoring occurred for me once when Martín Prechtel and I were driving down St. Charles Avenue one Sunday morning in New Orleans. We both took

---

[†] Clarence was the prisoner at DCI who first told me of growing up with the belief that prison is where a boy goes to become a man.

notice of a homeless man walking in the same direction as we were headed. He was tall, walked with a wandering and troubled gait, and wore a long, gray wool military coat with a flop-eared military hat the same color. I was struck by how sooty and dirty he and his clothes were, as if he had been working in a coal mine. I could not distinguish soot from beard on his face, which held the image of ultimate despair. As I looked away from him to drive, I could see that Martín continued to watch this person, who was strange looking even by homeless standards. When he finally turned back in his seat, he said rather matter-of-factly, "Ah, I think that was God back there."

"What do you mean?" I asked.

"When God comes down here, that's the way He looks sometimes," he answered.

A couple of weeks later, driving along that same part of St. Charles, I noticed a man standing at the intersection ahead. As the light changed to red, I slowed to a stop and read the sign he held. It said, "homeless." He did not share the striking features of the sooty man in the military coat I'd seen before. He appeared like most of the homeless people I had passed by over the last decade or so, when the homeless first began to appear on our streets.

The car in front of me stopped adjacent to the man but no one responded to his message. I had stuffed a couple of dollars and some change into my car console when buying breakfast on the way to the office. I grabbed the two bills and waited for the light to change. As I pulled forward, I lowered the window and offered the man the money. He took it and thanked me. As I glanced up at his face, the eyes I looked into did not look human. They were dark, but describing their color would not help to explain their essence. Far beyond gratitude, there was a profound blessing in them that was beyond my ability to express.

Subsequently, I began to keep more money at hand to offer the homeless, but after that first encounter, I saw only lost, lonely and deadened eyes. Many times the person would look away and not even offer a "thanks." That is all right. I can only imagine the intense humiliation a person must feel when begging on the streets. It's not free money—they pay the terrible price of their dignity. Besides, the memory of that intense blessing once received was enough to keep me giving and watching.

A year or so later, I found myself in Destin, Florida, where I had accompanied Rosie to a conference of district attorneys. She was to deliver a paper on the efficacy of diverting first-time drug offenders into treatment rather than prosecuting them and sending them to prison. The conference was at a resort called Sandestin, just a few miles from Destin, which is famous for its white-sand beaches and clear, blue-green waters.

We stopped to get cash at an ATM when a man in a pickup truck pulled in behind us. As the door of the pickup opened, I heard a beer can fall to the pavement. Turning around to check him out, I saw the archetypal image of the Southern redneck bend over, pick up the beer can, throw it back onto the floor of the truck and slam the door. *Oh, God,* I thought as I fired my arrows of disgust at the gut that hung from under his T-shirt and over his belt. *He would just love the ideas expressed by the conference of prosecutors we've just come from.*

I took my receipt for the withdrawal, retrieved my debit card and took a wider swath than necessary around him. As I swung past him, he said loudly in a thick southern brogue, "Hot, huh!" Glancing his way, I was stopped dead in my tracks because I was seeing those same eyes that had belonged to the homeless beggar on St. Charles Avenue. This time, though, they were blue and winked at me through thick-glassed spectacles as if to say, "Gotcha . . . and that'll teach ya'." In spite of being caught with my prejudicial pants down, I felt as blessed by him as if he had said to me, "It's okay." I share this mentoring story with all my students at Project Return, and it is one of their favorites.

A final, but most important, detail about my work during the past twelve years is that my learning curve has never peaked, although the shift from DCI to Project Return has changed the character of what I am learning. At DCI, I learned mostly about the criminal's life in prison, whereas at Project Return, I have learned mostly about the criminal's life

on the streets. In both cases, I had to completely scrap everything I thought I knew, which was mostly garnered from the
media. Trying to understand what criminals are like by watching television is as ridiculous as a man trying to understand
what women are like by watching television. Some in the
media would have us believe that every criminal is subhuman
or evil. Others try to say that criminals lead lives of intrigue,
excitement, glamour, fast cars and beautiful women. Neither
is fundamentally true.

In New Orleans, a typical criminal is chronically paranoid
about being recognized or caught, and he is forever desperate
about where he can safely sleep, where he can steal some
money or find his next fix. He gets up every morning by four
and is out on the street before five, because that's when the
police typically begin their raids. He does not watch television, or if he does, he must keep the sound turned down so he
can hear the bumps in the darkness outside. When he hears a
bump, his paranoia, already exacerbated by the crack cocaine
he has smoked, spikes completely off the scale. One woman
told us recently that when the cops finally came to arrest her,
"They cuffed me and put me in the back seat of the car, and I
rested my head against the window and said, 'Thank God.'" I
have heard so many people assume in such cases, "Well, she
just wanted to go back to prison," or "She didn't want to stop
using badly enough." They are dead wrong. Her addiction was
so completely out of control that she welcomed even the

dread of prison to the horrifying freefall of her drug abuse. In twelve years of listening to the stories of former offenders, I have never met one person who wanted to return to prison or who truly enjoyed criminal life.

These ongoing stories have advanced our learning curve at Project Return, stimulated our imaginations and generated a great deal of knowledge in the field of criminal justice. This was possible due to the particular approach we took toward our research. In general, scientists who want to study a group of people will simply ask questions, perhaps offer a certain stimulus like money, and then write down their observations. The idea is to remain separate from those whom they are observing and, thus, objective. Unfortunately, under this system any new knowledge is very limited. It is like writing about a perfume one has never smelled or a cake that has not been tasted.

Instead of taking this conventional approach, I chose to become deeply connected to it. When I became the student of those I observed as well as their teacher, I was transformed as much as they were. Did this affect my objectivity? Of course it did. So when I teach about my work, I have to work a little harder to remain objective. But it also means that I can speak about my work to more people than just scientists. I address moralists, judges, politicians, CEOs, Republicans and Democrats, preachers and atheists. To do that, one must have a much deeper understanding about one's subject.

If it is true that the more we participate in the observed culture the more new knowledge becomes available from the work, then there are implications regarding our approach to education, especially if we want our youth to grasp what is actually going on in the world around them. For example, if we want children to learn about poverty and ways of effectively addressing it, we must help them to become involved with those who live in poverty. Obviously, this cannot be done in a classroom or learned from a textbook, but it can be done, for instance, by *serving* those who are poor. The emphasis is on *serving*, not *helping*. This was clarified best by an aboriginal woman imprisoned in Australia who said, "If you came here to help, you are wasting your time. But if you are here because your own liberation is bound up with mine, then we have work to do."

In many of the myths and fairy tales where a prince or a princess is about to become a king or queen, the young protagonist has to first learn about poverty by *participating* in it. In the Grimm fairy tale *Iron John*, as retold by Robert Bly in his book of the same title, a mentor tells the young prince that he has a head of gold, (which means, perhaps, that he has a good education), but that he knows nothing of poverty. He tells the prince that to become a truly noble king, the next step on his journey is to work in the kitchen of the castle shoveling ashes. Cinderella, too, shoveled *cinders* before finding her prince. And so must we, if we are ever to find our own inner king/queen energy with which to actively and effectively resist the wrongs in our culture.

Another thing this work has taught us is that many men and women who have been in prison and have healed their wounds now represent a profound, untapped resource as mentors. This resource could help with many of society's problems in the areas of crime, drug and alcohol addictions, violence, and, in particular, youth at risk. While not all of our program's graduates could or should serve as mentors, many of them are in a unique position to help gang members and other adolescents with their problem behaviors. Former offenders have a unique capacity for relating to the problems of today's troubled youth, because they speak the language of poverty, hopelessness, parental neglect, physical abuse and sexual abuse. They, too, have grown up in violent neighborhoods, faced the temptations of drugs, and lost loved ones and friends to violence. For these reasons, they are powerful role models for change and transformation. Most important, they empathize with these young people's situations on a far deeper level than those of us with less experience and less understanding of life on the streets.

Today, every new story the men and women bring to Project Return teaches me something about the world. I was so moved by one story told during a workshop in Tennessee that I paraphrased it into my first published poem, *Raised by Drunks, Junk Dealers and Thieves*.

I did my time on my own—
Ain't nobody sent me no money.
I wash'd clothes, cleaned out cells for my dope.
Got ganged 4 or 5 times.
Down seb'mteen years—
Seb'mteen years o' 'Count time!! Chow time!! Work time!! Ball Field!!'
People yellin' at me—tellin' me what to do—
Seb'mteen years without a visit, er a letter, er nothin'.
Now, I'm lost. I don't know what to do but git drunk—
'at's only time I kin till my daddy I love him—
Sober, cain't say a word to him.
Ain't after that 6th beer neither—
't's after that 24th 'n—when I'm in that 2nd case.
But, then no one likes me—even if I'm sayin' 'I love you.'
Cain't talk about my feelin's though, 'less I'm drunk.
(pause)
"I ain't never had no one to talk to like this."

This poem's inspiration was a thirty-four-year-old man, Ray Beasley, who spent seventeen years in a Tennessee prison without a visit or even a letter. Shortly before his release, however, he heard from a childhood sweetheart. While giving him a ride home from prison, she agreed to begin seeing him again—his first ray of hope for a future life in two decades. The next day, she was killed in an auto accident, leaving him lost and not knowing how to handle his pain, except to stay drunk.

I sent the poem to Tim Dempsey, executive director of Chattanooga Endeavors, an ex-offender program in Tennessee that has adopted the key elements of Project Return's program design. Tim agreed to pass the poem on to Ray, who had gone there for help. When he did so, Ray looked at it and tucked it away in his pocket. "Did you read it?" Tim asked. When Ray shook his head, Tim realized he could not read and offered to read it for him. The very thought that anyone would care for him enough to write a poem based on his own words moved Ray deeply.

Some weeks later, a letter from Tim arrived. "Ray became suicidal today and I've hospitalized him. Please keep him in your prayers. And me too! There's a lot of pressure from those around me—speaking the voice of reason—to give up on him. I have no intention of doing that but wonder where such commitment will take me."

Tim's subsequent letter said that Ray was doing well. He went back to jail for a short sentence after his time in the mental hospital and is working installing gutters on houses. Ray is, of course, in my prayers. But also, in my words of gratitude, I thank God for quiet heroes like Tim Dempsey.

These stories never cease to take us down into the darkest places of grief and sometimes horror. But the most overwhelming truth about them comes from their awe-inspiring ability to bring people together into community across the barriers of race, religion, gender, politics and centuries of cultural separation. They provide the most compelling evidence that all people in all cultures are inescapably interconnected. Whatever happens to one affects all others, as Chief Seattle noted:

> *Man did not weave the web of life,*
> *He is merely a strand in it.*
> *Whatever he does to the web, he does to himself.*

This was intensely brought to light at one of the Men's Conferences in Minnesota a few years ago, where 150 of us were listening to Martín teach on the subject of initiation as his culture has practiced it for millennia. He was preparing us to participate in a ritual of initiation that would allow us to see the tip of the iceberg of what, down through the ages, has brought those young Mayan men safely into the beauty, the gentleness and the fierceness of responsible manhood.

A man stood up and said, and I paraphrase:

"I'm from Kansas City and I've always had a deep love for the Earth. It's been an amazing time for me to be here. But yesterday, I was thinking that, as a culture, we've destroyed an amazingly sophisticated, rhythmic nation, and I feel like I'm up here continuing the rip-off. Here I am, a white guy who's going to 'make my hoop' and what am I gonna do with it? I mean, I'm really glad, Martín, that I'm here and I'm glad you are here overseeing this. Because if it were some white guy up there who took the name 'Buffalo Sun' and was taking me into a sweat lodge to teach me the Indian ways, I wouldn't be able to hang with it. I mean, I read Gary Snyder and hear stories about the trickster and it's amazing. But I just wonder, can I as an Anglo white guy with a connective bloodstream to people who literally blasted these folks off the map, just waltz in and put on these clothes and turn the mask around? I'm in this ghost space that is at the same time beautiful, but . . ."

Martín interrupted and, again I paraphrase, said:

"Okay, you better come over here, 'cause this is something that has to be addressed. We can't just let it lay, 'cause then we'd be doing the white man thing, you know."

The man walked up to the front of the room where Martín turned him to face the crowd and stood behind him. He wrapped his arms around him as he spoke.

Martín continued, "So, you're still talking from that position of separatism. In other words, my people did this to these people; my people did this to that land. This whole Earth is your body; and you are a little person running around on this Earth. But that body of the land, which has been cut and maimed and mined and thrown around and treated as an extraneous object, is your own body and your own soul. And what you walk through in those mines and those wastelands of your body is the geography of the soul.

"So when you say to an Indian that you are sorry for killing our lands, you're still talking like a white man. You must realize that this body here is The Body, and that the indigenous person who sits inside you is on a reservation somewhere inside this body, isolated. And this indigenous person, the one we're addressing in these rituals, wants to come out; wants to come jumping out. . . . It is from an ancient place in every man, not just in the Indians. And as long as you see it as 'My people did this and my people did that, or your people did this and your people did that,' it shoots arrows into the heart of the indigenous person inside."

In my years of teaching life skills to the men and women who have come to Project Return, I have always included the message of this interconnected web in which we exist. What it comes down to for me in everyday life is this: I cannot harm another without harming myself in a worse way; I cannot steal something without losing something of greater value from within myself; a culture cannot oppress another without suffering greater oppression itself.

Not long after the experience with Martín, I listened to an interview of the Dalai Lama in which he was asked about his own capacity for compassion. Compassion, of course, is the underlying principle of the Dalai Lama's religion, his culture, indeed his entire life. The correspondent asked him,

"Considering all the destruction, the slaughter and the rape your people have suffered at the hands of the Red Chinese over the last fifty years, can you honestly tell me that you have compassion for the Communists of Red China?"

The Dalai Lama answered, "If you understood the profoundness with which we are all interconnected, you would understand that no one has suffered more than the Red Chinese. And how could I not have compassion for someone suffering that much?"

Suddenly, my thoughts went directly to one man—Warden Cain at DCI. I was immediately aware that he must suffer more than most people on Earth, and that I, in order to become fully human, must learn to replace my incredible anger for him with compassion. As soon as I made the decision to do so, I became aware also that Cain and others like him are not my greatest enemy.

My greatest enemy is ignorance—my own and that of others. It is out of ignorance that our culture writes off the millions of men and women in prison, blaming only them for all of society's troubles. It is out of ignorance that our culture views prisoners as one dangerous, homogenous lump and not as individuals, each with a story in which all of us have in some way participated. It was out of that ignorance that our president and many others once wrote letters to the government of Indonesia to save a young American boy from being caned, while we allow in our own prisons beatings that make such canings look like child's play. Finally, it is because of ignorance that the cruelty we abhor in our young is learned from the cruelty we ordain throughout our culture, such as that found in our prisons, and that so much suffering descends upon us from the suffering to which we have given our consent.

> *The most securely imprisoned population that exists is the general public that is uninformed about the nature and consequences of imprisonment as practiced in America today. They are imprisoned in a mass delusion, which, in the long run, punishes society far more severely than society can ever punish a convicted criminal.*
>
> KARL MENNINGER (1971)

When the light of understanding has overcome the darkness of ignorance, hopefully enough people will cry out for an end to the brutality in our prisons and that system will crumble as the Berlin Wall and South African apartheid crumbled. To conquer our ignorance, however, we will have to surrender our innocence.

It is to that end that I have written down these stories. My prayer is that they will offer another way to think about the part of our population that fills our prisons, a more practical, realistic, respectful and forward-thinking way that stresses the rebuilding of lives and the reclaiming of human resources. It must be a way that looks with compassion upon all whose lives have been forever changed by crime—the victims of crime and their families, those who are imprisoned and brutalized by our system of corrections, and their families who must suffer anguish and worry every night for the safety of their loved ones.

The promise of this book is that we are powerful beyond our imagination and can effect dramatic change toward harmony in our culture. We have everything to gain by trying.

Kindness

Before you know what kindness really is
you must lose things,
feel the future dissolve in a moment
like salt in a weakened broth.
What you held in your hand,
what you counted and carefully saved,
all this must go so you know
how desolate the landscape can be
between the regions of kindness.

Before you learn the tender gravity of kindness,
you must travel where the Indian in the white poncho
lies dead by the side of the road.
You must see how this could be you,
how he too was someone
who journeyed through the night with plans
and the simple breath that kept him alive.

Before you know kindness as the deepest thing inside,
you must know sorrow as the other deepest thing.
You must wake up with sorrow.
You must speak to it till your voice
catches the thread of all sorrows
and you see the size of the cloth.

Then it is only kindness that makes sense anymore,
only kindness that ties your shoes
and sends you out into the day to mail letters and purchase bread,
only kindness that raises it head
from the crowd of the world to say,
"It is I you have been looking for,"
and then goes with you everywhere
like a shadow or a friend.

NAOMI SHIHAB NYE

Epilogue: A Sad Farewell and a New Beginning

*L*ast December, tragedy struck. Malcolm's son, Gerard, took part in the armed robbery of a pawnshop. He had for some time been keeping company with a slightly older and very charismatic rapper who had apparently convinced Gerard to resist his better judgment and enter the same life of crime that had caused his father so much suffering. Malcolm and I knew nothing about it until we heard that the police had raided Gerard's mother's house early one morning and discovered practically everything that had been taken from the shop except for some guns and jewelry. Meanwhile, Gerard became a fugitive. When he later called Malcolm from a pay phone, Malcolm begged him to turn himself in, but, regrettably, he refused. This, of course, devastated Malcolm.

In the middle of this crisis, Malcolm's older brother, Jacob, died of a lengthy illness. Everyone on the Project Return staff drove up to New Iberia, Louisiana, for the funeral. Rosie's mother, Helen, whom Malcolm has called Sister Helen since she used to send letters and small gifts to him in prison, asked to go along. She was eighty-nine years old and in a wheel-chair. Malcolm spoke about his brother for the family. He told the gathering that although Jacob was quite the most obstinate person he'd ever known, he also had been devoted to Malcolm as a brother. He spoke of how Jacob had helped him numerous times during his desperate days in Houston when Malcolm was struggling to stay in a Job Corps program and resist the temptation to slip back into the life of crime and drugs.

Following the funeral, we all went to the home of Malcolm's mother, Eunice. There, Sister Helen and Eunice met face-to-face for the first time. They, too, had corresponded during those last years of Malcolm's imprisonment. Helen broke into tears when they met, saying, "I didn't think I was going to live long enough to meet you." This beautiful encounter between these two elder women brought considerable joy to a very sad occasion.

A few days after the funeral, Malcolm returned to New Orleans. Already exhausted from many months of too much work, he initially went into a deep depression and, not long after, relapsed into drug use after fourteen years of being clean and sober. I failed to catch the first signs of Malcolm's relapse. At first, he began missing more and more hours from work, then he lost a noticeable amount of weight. Finally, he frantically began taking on more and more tasks to help other people until he reached the point of total collapse. By the time all of these symptoms collectively woke me up, it was too late for me to engage in simple confrontations and take appropriate counter measures. Malcolm had descended into a complete psychotic break, and the dear friend I had come to know and love was no longer present. When I was at last able to catch up with him, at his house, it seemed to me that he was possessed by a demon, so uncharacteristic was his behavior. His emotional affect was completely flat, his language seemed to have returned to the street, and I remember noting that this was the first time I had ever seen him with a cigarette. When I said that I wanted to help him and that we could work things out so he could return to his job, he told me that he fully intended to leave town and disappear. My entire staff agreed to gather outside of his house for a group intervention, with the goal of urging him to confront his condition and coaxing him into a treatment program. Malcolm refused to speak to them as well. No amount of logic or persuasion could penetrate his addiction. Whatever force or energy possessed him did not care that he would lose the home he had struggled to purchase, that his daughter would have no place to live, and that his son would not have the help that Malcolm could provide in the struggle he would eventually face.

A few weeks later, Malcolm's sister died unexpectedly from a heart attack. Malcolm called me at home and asked if Rosie and I would drive up for her funeral, but when we arrived at the church, no one was there. Driving toward Eunice's house, we happened to see Malcolm drying off his car at a car wash and pulled over to talk to him. He was wearing a green warm-up suit, had a cigarette in his mouth and looked as though he had lost half his body weight. I felt heartsick to see him like this. His demeanor was friendly but jittery as he told us he really wasn't sure what time the funeral started—possibly in a couple of hours.

A bit perturbed since we had both cancelled important meetings, gotten up very early and fought rush-hour traffic in New Orleans and Baton Rouge to get to New Iberia in time, Rosie and I drove to the local Dairy Queen to wait. By noon, the family still had not appeared for the funeral, so we decided to simply wait outside the church, greet Malcolm and his mother, and then head on back to New Orleans. Soon, the limousine arrived from which Eunice emerged, appearing shattered by everything that had happened. We waited another half-hour before Malcolm showed up, looking, despite his weight loss, handsome and noble as ever in his suit. We said our sad farewells. Since that afternoon, I have seen him but once and do not know how to contact him.

When Rosie's mother, Helen, died a few years later, he left word at her office expressing his sorrow. With all my training and experience, I could speculate on a thousand reasons that might explain why this happened and I would still not know the entire truth. If language cannot touch the essence of our friendship, neither can it adequately assess Malcolm's affliction. Still, there were two things I felt that I had to do. One was to take a hard look at my own mistakes, and the other was to find some kind of meaning in what had occurred.

Martín Prechtel pointed out to me that no one ever guaranteed that, in leaving my former career and devoting myself to this work, I would emerge "intact."

The poet Rilke said that perhaps being defeated like this might even be the ultimate goal of our lessons in surrendering our lives to Divine will. Referring to the angel who appeared to the wrestlers of the Old Testament, he said:

> *When the wrestlers' sinews grew long like metal strings, he felt them under his fingers like chords of deep music. Whoever was beaten by this Angel went away proud and strengthened and great from that harsh hand that kneaded him as if to change his shape. Winning does not tempt that man. This is how he grows: by being defeated, decisively, by constantly greater beings."*[7]

However, the most important lesson to be learned from this sad episode is not that I am strengthened by tragedy, but that, in spite of all that has happened, Project Return remains intact. The amount of time I have had to take away from my normal duties and devote to the problems which Malcolm's departure presented me, as well as other pressing matters, has been considerable. And yet, the work itself has continued to flourish. In fact, I can say without hesitation that my entire staff has been strengthened by this "defeat." They have all taken on Malcolm's tasks and responsibilities, such as working with judges, parole and probation officers, and juvenile authorities, as well as addressing the personal problems of our participants. Each of them has learned new skills, discovered talents and enjoyed new kinds of successes in completing these tasks.

Perhaps the greatest value of this experience has been to teach us that the concepts of compassion, responsibility, reconciliation and forgiveness[8]—and of providing for the needs of people in desperate circumstances—give this work a life of its own that will continue to grow long after Malcolm *and* I are dead. Love and compassion are what created Project Return and these spirits alone will keep it alive.

The last time I talked to Malcolm, I told him that I would write about this, and that I would never regret the ten years he and I had known each other, worked, traveled, laughed and wept together. I am a better man, more of a man, because of those years with him. And, in part because of that, my four sons are better men. For that, I will be forever grateful to him and my prayers will always include him, in the wish that perhaps we may meet again somewhere in time.

———

A few months ago, Rosie and I attended a lecture by Sister Helen Prejean and Father Daniel Berrigan at Loyola University in New Orleans. The two were brilliant together as they spoke of the violence that pervades our culture and the difficult issues that surround the death penalty. Later in the evening, as they were fielding questions from the audience, I heard a young man's voice expressing praise and gratitude to Sister Helen for the work she had done over the years at Angola. He said that he had spent seventeen years at Angola and, though he had never seen her personally, word of her visits and her compassion for those in prison spread throughout the numerous compounds at Angola, giving hope to many that someone still valued them as human beings.

The voice belonged to John La Fleur, who had attended the Minnesota Men's Conference with us when Peyton was killed. John went on to describe how he had turned his life around after graduating from Project Return. He spoke about finding a job and settling into a new, productive life, with plans to marry the next year. Following his comments, he received warm and enthusiastic applause from the audience of over one thousand.

During the applause, I remembered a phone call from John a few months earlier. He wanted to tell me a story about his new pickup truck and the construction job he had recently completed—building a parking garage in downtown New Orleans. During the last week of construction, he had received permission from his boss to take a day of leave on the coming Friday. Thursday of that same week happened to be his last day of parole and, for the first time in twenty-four years, since he was fourteen years old, John could legally leave town and the state without filing for official approval. Early on Friday morning, he headed north without a plan or destination in mind. He spent the first night of his new freedom on a mountain somewhere in Tennessee and, before heading south again to report for work on Monday, he slept on the shore of Lake Michigan.

When the applause settled and the auditorium was quiet, Sister Prejean asked us, "Gosh, is there anything sweeter or more beautiful than listening to someone who has transformed his life?" As the audience applauded again, I thought to myself, *No, I do not think there is.*

My fiftieth year had come and gone,
I sat, a solitary man,
In a crowded London shop,
An open book and empty cup
On the marble table-top.
While on the shop and street I gazed
My body of a sudden blazed;
And twenty minutes more or less
It seemed, so great my happiness,
That I was blessed and could bless.

WILLIAM BUTLER YEATS

Postscript

*T*his unlikely journey has restored beauty to "my garden," but seems far from ending. It has led me further
still into the indigenous world—four times into mysterious
Africa and the village of my mentor, Malidoma Somé.

Notes

[1] Overview of the Community-Building Model

Participants gather in a circle for two or three eight-hour days, having in mind a single goal or commitment to become a "true community." The workshop is entirely experiential; that is, the members of the group do not receive instructions on how to become a community or how to behave in a community. Peck's reasoning is that passive learning, while easy, is almost invariably shallow; experiential learning, on the other hand, although demanding, is infinitely more profound and rewarding. In accordance with the community-building model, only a few "ground rules" regarding communication and commitment are offered by workshop leaders:

(a) Each participant is responsible for the success of the task.

(b) Participants should voice their displeasure within the group process and share these feelings with the entire group, not to individuals during the breaks.

(c) The group must commit to "hang in" through periods of anxiety, frustration, doubt, anger, depression and even despair, which may be expected on the way to community.

(d) The group must be committed to confidentiality.

(e) Other procedural norms, such as punctuality, the wearing of name tags and stating one's name prior to speaking, are established by the two workshop facilitators.

(f) Participants are told by the two workshop facilitators that two of the greatest barriers to communication are speaking when one is not moved to do so and failing to speak when one is so moved.

Next, a story that is a metaphor for community building is read to the circle of participants. This is followed by three minutes of silence. Then the community-building process begins.

Though each group is unique, a pattern of progressive and essential stages in the community-building process is identifiable:

(a) Pseudo-community. This is characterized by politeness, avoidance of overt disagreement, denying individual differences, beliefs that a "community" already exists, an indifference/resistance to the goal of building a community and lack of assertion of feelings. These feelings are often anger and paranoia about being there (nonvoluntarily), genuine curiosity and hopeful interest, or fear and confusion.

(b) Chaos. In this stage, open conflict can be quite apparent with attempts to "heal and convert" others into adopting a particular way of thinking. To end the chaos, some groups will attempt to organize into subgroups or structured discussion, which is incompatible with developing community.

(c) Emptiness. This stage is the bridge to community. Emptiness refers to the difficult task of letting go of one's barriers to community. These barriers are commonly things such as expectations and preconceptions about the group, prejudices, or the need to fix or control the group or to appear to "have it all together." The experience of recognizing and letting go of these barriers is called "group death."

(d) Community. Once the group has completed the task of emptiness, it enters community. It is during this stage that the dynamics of the group change. Characteristics such as the expression of and respect for individual differences, shared leadership, spontaneity, quietness, joy, commitment to embracing painful realities and the ability to begin thinking about the health of the group as a whole can emerge.

² U.S. Justice Department officials who wrote the federal requirements for prisons doing business with the private sector had concerns that prisons would abuse the opportunity for such enterprises. Their federal mandate was twofold. First, they were to provide prisoners with a valuable trade in these jobs that could serve them in obtaining employment upon release from prison. Second, they were to ensure that prisoners were paid minimum wages while performing prison jobs so they would have at least some money on which to survive at the time of their release.

A Justice Department official told me that Louisiana's Prison Enterprises made their worst fears come true at DCI. There, Prison Enterprises operated a crawfish/onion plant that was represented to the media as a vocational/educational program. The only thing a prisoner who worked there could learn was how to boil onions and peel crawfish tails. Moreover, I was told that the minimum wages the men were supposed to receive were diverted into an account called the Inmate Welfare Fund, which is under the control of the warden. Later, I heard that when the U.S. Department of Justice officials learned about the operation, they closed it down.

Media sources in Louisiana reported in 1997 that Warden Burl Cain had spent money from this fund at Angola to construct a pier on the prison lake from which he and other officials could fish. They also reported that Warden Cain closed a Department of Labor–sponsored auto body/mechanic school at DCI and rewrote the grant to open a farrier school (for shoeing horses). The warden reportedly did a lot of trading in horses as a hobby. So much for education and rehabilitation.

³ For over forty years, Robert Bly has held a place among the foremost poets of his generation, while positioning himself as an outsider in both the larger society, which he sees as dominated by consumerist culture, and the literary community, which he feels is dominated by the academy. Unlike most of America's prominent poets, Bly has eschewed university teaching, preferring to live in the small town of Moose Lake, Minnesota—the state he was born in—on a farm with his wife and three children. He makes his living writing, giving poetry readings around the nation and translating Scandinavian fiction. He has also worked extensively as an editor. Bly's poetry is characterized by free association, and often concerns the hidden connections between the natural world and

the human mind. In 1990, Bly made something of a departure from poetry with the publication of *Iron John: A Book About Men,* a nonfiction work that received much media attention. The book concerns the ancient rituals and traditional myths humanity has used to connect with the masculine side of nature. In *Iron John,* Bly argues that contemporary men are out of touch with their own masculinity, an estrangement that causes tremendous grief and alienation. Though this project was quite different from his previous publications, the subject was not exactly new to Bly; he had been leading seminars for men for more than ten years.

[4] Since what Robert Bly prefers to call "The Men's Mytho-poetical movement" was founded by men who are, either literally or spiritually, poets and storytellers, it is not surprising that the hard and passionate truths of poetry are very important to the movement. After that meeting, I began to jot down bits of poetry that dealt with the taming of violence. One by Rumi caught the essence of chaos and conflict:

One Dervish to another,
What was your vision of God's presence?
I haven't seen anything.
But for the sake of conversation, I'll tell you a story.
God's presence is there in front of me, a fire on the left, a lovely stream on
    the right.
One group walks toward the fire, into the fire, another toward the sweet
    flowing water.
No one knows which are blessed and which not.
Whoever walks into the fire appears suddenly in the stream.
A head goes under on the water surface, that head pokes out of the fire.
Most people guard against going into the fire,
and so end up in it.
Those who love the water of pleasure and make it their devotion are cheated
    with this reversal.
The trickery goes further.
The voice of the fire tells the truth, saying I am not fire.
I am fountainhead. Come into me and don't mind the sparks.

                                (translated by Coleman Banks)

[5] Mirabai, mystic and poet, India's most famous medieval saint. A Rajput princess, married to the crown prince of Mewar, she refused to immolate herself on her husband's funeral pyre when he died. She flouted Hindu customs in many other ways; absorbed in her devotion to Krishna, she spent all her time at the temple, singing and dancing before his image, and mingling with the male devotees. Eventually, fed up with her family's harassment, she became a wandering ascetic feeding the poor. Her songs, like Kabir's, are still sung by the common people throughout India. "My teacher taught me this," she said, "Approve me or disapprove me. I praise the mountain's energy night and day. I walk the path that ecstatic people have walked for centuries. I don't steal anything. I don't hit anyone. With what will you charge me? I have felt the swaying of the elephant's shoulders. And you would have me climb on a jackass. Try to be serious." (Translated by Robert Bly.)

[6] Dagara Prayer

Greetings Ancestor Spirits, Greetings Spirit Guides, Friends of the Invisible. You who know without learning, you who see without looking, I have come to tell you that I am about to go on a journey. But how can a blind man travel? My eyes can't show me the way, my feet can't hold me, and my wit won't show me through the traps. So I give myself away to you, that you may be my eyes, and my feet and my wit. That I may see through you and walk beside you and feel your presence. For it is only through you that this journey can happen as a journey. May it be a safe one.

[7] The Man Watching

> I can tell by the way the trees beat, after
> so many dull days, on my worried windowpanes
> that a storm is coming,
> and I hear the far off fields say things
> I can't bear without a friend,
> I can't love without a sister.

The storm, the shifter of shapes, drives on
across the woods and across time,
and the world looks as if it had no age:
the landscape, like a line in the psalm book,
is seriousness and weight and eternity.

What we choose to fight is so tiny!
What fights with us is so great!
If only we would let ourselves be dominated
as things do by some immense storm,
we would become strong too, and not need names.
When we win it's with small things,
and the triumph itself makes us small.
What is extraordinary and eternal
does not want to be bent by us.
I mean the Angel who appeared
to the wrestlers of the Old Testament:
when the wrestlers' sinews
grew long like metal strings,
he felt them under his fingers
like chords of deep music.

Whoever was beaten by this Angel
(who often simply declined the fight)
went away proud and strengthened
and great from that harsh hand,
that kneaded him as if to change his shape.
Winning does not temp that man.
This is how he grows: by being defeated, decisively,
by constantly greater beings.

                              Rainer Maria Rilke (translated by Robert Bly)

[8] from *We're All Doing Time*

> Every great spiritual, philosophic and religious tradition has empha-
> sized compassion, reconciliation, forgiveness and responsibility. These
> are not suggestions, they are instructions. If we follow them we will
> thrive, if not we will suffer.
>
> Bo Lozoff

Pure Inspiration

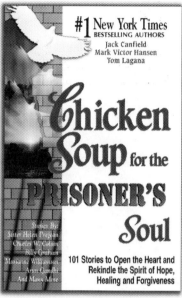

Code #8369 •Paperback • $12.95

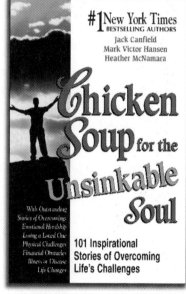

These books will leave an indelible imprint on your heart and inspire you to live with hope, gratitude and joy.

Code #6986 •Paperback • $12.95